A
House
United

A
House
United

How Christ-Centered Unity
Can End Church Division

Francis Frangipane

Chosen
Grand Rapids, Michigan

© 2002, 2005 by Francis Frangipane

Published by Chosen Books
a division of Baker Publishing Group
P. O. Box 6287, Grand Rapids, MI 49516-6287
www.chosenbooks.com

Second printing, June 2006

Revised and expanded from an earlier book entitled *It's Time to End Church Splits*, © 2002 by Francis Frangipane, published by Arrow Publications, Cedar Rapids, IA

Printed in the United States of America

Library of Congress Cataloging-in-Publication Data
Frangipane, Francis.
A house united : how Christ-centered unity can end church division / Francis Frangipane.
    p.   cm.
    ISBN 10: 0-8007-9397-8 (pbk.)
    ISBN 978-0-8007-9397-5 (pbk.)
    1. Church controversies. 2. Church—Unity. 3. Schism. I. Title.
BV652.9.F73 2006
250—dc22   2005028227

This book is dedicated to all those who have been wounded by the heartache of a church split.

May the Lord touch, heal and empower each heart to stand for Christ-centered unity in the house of the Lord.

Contents

Part 4 Becoming Christlike

Part 5 The Gate of Heaven

Introduction

The Bible tells us that Jesus Christ is the same yesterday, today and forever (see Hebrews 13:8). Just as He prayed that His early disciples would become one, so He also prayed for unity among His people today. Remember His prayer? He said, "I do not ask on behalf of these alone, but for those also who believe in Me through their word; that they may all be one" (John 17:20–21).

It is obvious that Jesus Christ passionately desires His people to be healed of the effects of splits and divisions. Indeed, the more I come to know the Lord's heart, the more I am convinced that disunity among the people of God is the work of hell. The curse of division has gone on long enough.

Thus, my deepest desire is to exalt the power and blessedness of Christ-centered unity. My goal, therefore, is to help shepherds and their flocks secure Christlikeness in their church relationships. If we find this holy, wonderful place, we also will discover that God's house is truly the gate of heaven (see Genesis 28:17).

Ending Division

I began this work focused on ending divisions and church splits among born-again Christians. There may be other books available on this subject, but I had not found any. Thus, to help me prioritize what I would put in this work, we asked those who receive our weekly email teaching to comment on the issue of church splits. Most of the responses I received were passionate and heartrending.

Approximately 60 percent of those who responded expressed a deep and ongoing grief because of what they had suffered in a church split. Of these, about 25 percent wrote long and painful responses, the majority describing how a discontented group within their congregation had divided and split what once was a loving church. A few of these emails were so painful they brought tears to my eyes. Within this group, the most common adjective used to describe the experience was the word *devastating*.

Quite a few said they had been through more than one split. Others were children when they experienced the division and described their extreme difficulty in returning to Christianity as adults. About 10 percent were cynical and critical. Their concern was that this might be another book justifying what they called the "abuse of authority." They expressed that their church divided because of the pastor's sin. They also complained that the lack of accountability in a few nondenominational churches let pastors become so authoritarian that the only "spiritual" thing left to do was to rebel and start a new assembly. Citing the Protestant reformers, a handful within this group felt the greatest Christians the Church has ever produced were those who confronted ungodly leaders.

A number of people presented complex situations that led to their church splitting. Others simply wanted to know what could be done to find healing, as the wounds of a split remained open within their hearts.

Obviously no one book could answer all these questions. Even if I tried, I do not think I would have the right answers to each of these situations. So I have sought to address the most common issues: the splits that are born of ambition in a subordinate pastor or worship leader, and the splits where the pastor himself divides the church or falls into serious sin. My goal is to help heal the hearts of pastors and congregations alike. I also desire to set some standards, or "Kingdom ethics," to help avoid this heartache in the future.

For those who are fearful that I am seeking to unite everyone who calls himself or herself Christian, I want to clarify that my appeal is to the born-again Church. Some of you are involved in trying to reconcile your role in denominational churches where the leaders are sanctioning homosexuality and other sins. Should you leave? This question is answered in the appendix at the back of the book, but addressing this subject in length is not my primary objective. My readers are primarily people who desire to become more Christlike. If you are reading this but do not desire to become like Jesus, you probably will not get far within these pages.

One last thing: If you are in the midst of a serious church division, I suggest you review the table of contents and start this book with the chapters that are most relevant to your current situation. Of course, you should return to the unread chapters, but it may be important for you to first assimilate the information that addresses your immediate conflict.

I realize that what I have presented here is quite inadequate. But let us unite in prayer, trusting God that He, in His grace, will raise up others to join this effort to end church splits and divisions. Let's take faith that, within our generation, we will see Christ's Church united and God's people healed of this curse of division and splits.

Part 1

The Sin of Division and Splits

And there was war in heaven. . . .
Revelation 12:7

The Great Division

> Lucifer's terrible crime was not simply that he rebelled against God, as evil as that was. Even worse, through slander against God and deception, he stole away a third of the angels as well. Though banished to hell, Lucifer's war against the Almighty continues. Indeed, every time he divides another church, he accomplishes part of his goal, which is to strike against the heart of God.

If you have ever been through a church split, you are all too familiar with the terrible churning of emotions and the inconsolable distress that accompanies this descent into hell. If you are unfamiliar with the experience, expect that large factions of otherwise nice Christians will be pitted against one another. They will participate in slander, anger, deception, fear, bitterness, hatred, gossip, unforgiveness, strife, rebellion and pride.

Any of these attitudes isolated in a single individual would be recognized and exposed as sin. But when they occur en masse in a church split, they somehow are considered righteous. Anger is redefined as "fighting for a principle." Slander and gossip now enlist as allies "in search of the truth."

The epicenter of the split may have been localized in a single church, but the shock waves are felt across the area-wide Body of Christ. News of the conflict is communicated in whispered tones, as when hearing of a family member who has a serious cancer. And a split is a cancer—a malignant life system, a false growth that is empowered by anger, pride and ambition instead of the meekness and patience of Christ.

Citywide church leaders shake their heads and sigh. Even if they barely knew the troubled church, they suffer sympathy pains. They are concerned. Those who have experienced the heartache of their own split shudder, as they remember the still unresolved conflict they carry regarding those who divided their church. Still other pastors become restless and more guarded over their flocks, wary lest the spirit of strife infiltrate their churches as well.

The evangelists of the city know that, at least for a season, it will be harder to win the lost. Indeed, as rumors and details of the split spread, the pettiness and politics reach the ears of the unsaved and remind them why they are keeping their distance from church.

I have traveled throughout most of the Christian world speaking to pastors and church leaders. It is my experience that, while divisions are found everywhere, splits are more frequent and often more mean-spirited in America. Is it our fierce love of independence and freedom? Or is it because of our more aggressive cultural nature? Regardless, American splits tend to have the least civility.

The reasons for church splits are many. Divisions may originate from confusion concerning church governments. To whom has God really given final authority in any given congregation? Sometimes the root of conflict is simply misguided ambition in one or more associate leaders. And of course, there is always the issue of spiritual warfare. Often, just as a church begins an upward swing in attendance or spiritual growth, demonically manipulated strife emerges. So when we see a serious division in a church, we must ask ourselves: Is this the work of the same kind of spirit that manipulated Absalom, Korah or Jezebel?

Some splits involve a combination of all the above. But regardless of the unique source of each division, Jesus warned that when a house is divided, it "will not stand" (Matthew 12:25). Clearly, when a division strikes a church, its impact is felt throughout the community. It is a war in which the devil is the only one who wins.

Heartache in Heaven

We may think the Lord is personally unfamiliar with the pain of a church split. He is not. In fact, pastors can take some comfort that God Himself, even in all His perfections, suffered a type of split. You may recall that before the creation of man, heaven endured a time of great rebellion—a "split," if you will.

In those days Satan was known as Lucifer, or *Hillel Ben Shahar*, in the Hebrew language. The name *Hillel* came from the root word *Hallel,* which meant "to praise, worship, adore." *Ben Shahar* meant "son of the dawn." The implication is that Lucifer was the chief worship leader at the dawn of creation. Endowed with the gifts of leadership and creativity in music, his position was not enough for him. Fueled by jealousy and ambition, Lucifer led a third of the angels to rebel against the authority of God (see Revelation 12). Ancient traditions say that Lucifer, together with Michael, Uriel and Gabriel, was one of the original archangels (see 2 Esdras 4). We cannot verify it, but we can imagine that the angels who fell were those who, in the authority structure of heaven, were under Lucifer.

Consider the cunning of Lucifer, our ancient foe. He was actually able to convince angels, who were gazing upon the resplendent glory of God, that they could win a war against their Creator! In privileged awe they had seen galaxies emerge from the mouth of God. Yet somehow they came to believe that under Lucifer's leadership they could defeat the Almighty.

They knew God was fully cognizant of their every thought, yet they believed they could outthink Him. Through stealth, slander and seduction, Lucifer weaved intoxicating lies to engender discontentment among the angels so that the very pleasures of heaven could not satisfy them. He then lured them from the unimaginable splendor of God's presence, convincing them the unfathomable outer darkness was more suited for their cause. Yes, consider the deceptive powers of our ancient foe and wonder not that he could separate good friends in a church split here on earth.

How long the rebellion in heaven lasted we do not know. Nor is it written what deception Lucifer spun. The Bible grants only fleeting reflections into that horrible, cataclysmic divide. Still one wonders: Did the Lord remain unaffected by the strife? Was the heavenly Father perfectly aloof from the pain of separation, or did He suffer heartache when those to whom He gave the gift of life rebelled against Him? Remember: God watched the great lie spread, infecting one angel after another, until a full third joined in the insurrection. Was this division the first great pain in the heart of God?

Beloved, consider also with trembling fear: Until this ancient split, to our knowledge hell did not exist. Hell became a reality as a consequence of division. It was created for those who believed the devil's lie (see Matthew 25:41).

In subsequent chapters we will look at some of the causes as well as some cures for divisions and splits. We will discuss Kingdom protocols and expose how the enemy can manipulate our religious ambitions. We also will look at healing a wounded church and restoring the broken pastor. We will even examine the rare times when God allows a split. For now, let us acknowledge that division and splits are serious sins. They remind God of when hell began.

Lord, forgive us for tolerating this terrible sin. Master, we know that our division is a blight upon Your people. Cleanse us of the effects of division, and empower each of us with grace to bring unity to Your Church. In Jesus' name. Amen.

The Issue Is Not the Issue

The Father has decreed that Christ's Church shall be united. His Son has purchased it, and the Holy Spirit is here to establish it. The battle you are facing is a distraction; the real issue is to maintain the oneness of Christ.

In the last chapter we marveled that heaven itself endured a time of strife, a war during which Lucifer challenged the authority and leadership of God. We also saw that hell was created as a result of the division in heaven. Yet although Lucifer and his hosts were banished to "pits of darkness" (2 Peter 2:4), their war with heaven did not end. Starting with Adam and Eve, the devil continued his war against God. The strife Christians experience today, in a real way, is a continuation of the great primeval conflict.

Recall also that when Lucifer lured the angels from God, he spoke such vile slander that glorious angels soon became hardened demons. While the Father knew beforehand of Lucifer's plans and rebellion, the fall of the angels must have grieved the Lord's heart. Yes, and our divisions, engendered by Satan, further strike against the heart of God.

One Who Divides

One truth that will help us defeat the enemy is knowing that when a church is suffering the heartbreak of division, what seems to be the issue is often not the issue at all. Indeed, when Lucifer fell, from heaven's standpoint he no longer retained the name Lucifer, but instead was called "Satan" or the "devil." The meanings of these two names give us a view into the nature of what we are fighting during a split.

Satan means "one who opposes" or "adversary." What power strengthens the confrontational attitude of those in opposition to the established church authority? What evil emboldens those who now disregard love, church order and civility to obtain their desires? The power reinforcing the inability to reconcile is satanic, and it can wedge itself between those in dissent and those in leadership. All sides must beware. Satan will fiercely oppose the idea of healing and reconciliation.

Let us also look at the name *devil*, which means "slanderer." To slander means more than "to speak evil of one to another." Speaking literally, it means "one who puts himself or something between two in order to divide them."

Satan's goal is not just to speak evil; it is to put something between people in order to divide them. This dividing work destroys friendships, marriages and churches. He will exaggerate what seems wrong in one person and twist the remarks of the other person's reaction. He will frustrate our attempts to compromise and will repeatedly divide Christians with new issues.

It is a mark of a church under demonic attack that the criticisms of the divisive group never let up; settle one issue and three more erupt. When Satan manipulates a splinter group within a church, the issues that inflame them cannot actually be satisfied. The pastor's answers do not satisfy, nor are attempts to compromise or find balance usually effective.

The issues rising between opposing camps are a smoke screen used by Satan to divide and conquer a church. They seem real enough, but when an issue becomes more central to a relationship than humility, love and faith, that issue is really a wedge sent to divide.

You see, the issue is not the color of the new carpet or the style of praise and worship or how long the sermon should be. The real issue is this: In spite of our differences, will we defend the unity of Christ within the fellowship?

Christ, the Unifying Factor

Just as the devil's goal is to put himself or something between people to divide them, so Christ puts Himself among us in order to heal us and bring unity. While He instructs us to honor our leaders within a church, He also tells us to prefer one another and submit to one another in holy fear. As we seek His forgiveness for our sins, He reminds us that to receive His forgiveness, we also must forgive others (see Matthew 6 and 18). And again, He decrees that if we are at the altar and there remember someone has something against us, we are to leave our offering and seek to be reconciled (see Matthew 5:23–24).

Additionally, the Lord puts His Spirit and His cross between us, reminding us that our issues are not the issue: *He is!* As Jonathan spoke in covenant with David, "May the LORD be between you and me . . . forever" (1 Samuel 20:42, NKJV). God places His Son between us, not issues. The only other issue we might ponder is: How can we, in this potential conflict, become examples to others of God's redemptive grace?

If You Are in a Split

When division strikes a church, three primary groups are usually involved. The first group consists of those who have initiated the division. They have issues with the leader or the pastoral team. They are discontent with the status quo and desire significant changes in the fellowship. The second group is the current senior leader and his staff who, though embattled, remain loyal to him or at least supportive of his position as pastor. The third group, usually the largest, is comprised of those caught in the middle of the division. These are the innocent sheep who have relationships with their leaders but are also friends with the dissenters. Hearing slander and rumors, they are confused and unsure of what to believe or whom to follow.

The dissenting group may use a smoke screen of religious issues to empower their cause: "We just want more of God." Or, "We want more freedom to grow." Such arguments seem both innocent and legitimate until we remember that anyone can seek God and enjoy more of Him at any time; there is no need to divide the church to have more of God's presence, especially since division itself causes God's manifest presence to withdraw!

As the conflict remains unresolved, two groups in the church, each with its own leaders, rise in opposition. Whom do you follow? To discern the true shepherd among you, recall the wisdom of Solomon. When two women came, each claiming a newborn as her own, as a test Solomon ordered the child to be split in two. The true mother begged that the child remain alive. The false mother, however, agreed to let the baby be split in two. Solomon recognized that the one who loved the child the most, the true mother, would not allow her baby to be divided. Thus, he recognized her parental love and awarded her with her offspring (see 1 Kings 3:16–27).

In your church, the true shepherd is the one who seeks to keep your church together. He will not initiate a split as a solution. He will not kill the baby by dividing it. He will seek to settle the legitimate issues while maintaining his focus on the higher issue of Christ-centered unity and healing.

I am not implying that there are not valid issues to discuss with church leaders. Nor am I saying that churches should not become more effective in ministry—some of the best ideas come from the congregation! I am stating only that the conflict that divides us is often a subterfuge from the enemy. The real issue is this: In spite of conflict, will we maintain meekness, love and unity? Will we, with Christlike integrity, defend the heart of God against Satan's quest to divide us?

Lord, forgive us for allowing divisions and splits to become such deeply ingrained traditions in Christianity. We confess that we are easily manipulated by false issues. Lord, make us instruments of healing. Help us to work with You to unite the Church and prepare Your Bride. Help us to see the real issue: In all our diversity, will we remain united? In Jesus' name. Amen.

When Little Ones Stumble

Nothing so offends the heart of God as when children or new believers stumble over the sin of those who knew better.

One of the most important reasons to avoid a church split, or to avoid opening ourselves up to anger and division, is the effect church conflicts have upon our children. The unresolved memory of a painful church split incubates long and silently in the souls of children. Though they outwardly continue in church attendance Sunday after Sunday with their parents, their wounded souls assign a minimal value to the benefits of church in general. When they are old enough, many young people walk away from church forever.

Thus, the most affected victims of church splits are the children. Inevitably, at some point during the conflict they hear their parents speaking angrily about the pastor or other church members. The children, who really have no part in the conflict, are now forced to take sides. With the parents of their beloved friends on the other side of the division, it is an unbearable injustice to inflict upon children of any age.

Let me reinforce the issue about causing little ones, or new believers, to stumble. To do so, I need to share with you how I came to Christ. My prayer is that God's people would learn the fear of the Lord and that at all costs we would avoid causing children to stumble.

The date was November 24, 1970. I was living in a farmhouse in the Blue Ridge Mountains of Virginia with about fourteen other people—all were Christians except one other person and myself. At that time of my life, I would not have called myself a pagan, but nearly all in the home would have. Actually, I considered myself an earnest seeker of God. During the years that the Lord was drawing me to Himself, though I did not know the Lord personally, I often felt the warm touch of His presence, so much so that I even referred to the interactive, wooing influence of the Holy Spirit as my *invisible friend.*

During these pre-Christian years, however, I also had amassed a lot of false information, which I compiled from many religions. So although I was sincerely seeking God, I had begun my quest by rejecting the denominational Christianity of my youth and blindly opening myself to Eastern religions and New Age teachers. The result was that I had developed my own private religion.

Wood stoves strategically placed in various rooms throughout the dwelling heated the farmhouse. One stove was to my immediate right, and it heated the dining room where I was sitting. On my left was a long dining room table from which I had pulled my chair to talk to the three novice Christians who were sitting on a couch against the wall. One by one they took turns witnessing to me. I not only deftly defended my views, but my self-made philosophy also began to undermine their faith.

"At their essence, all religions are the same," I said. "Each in its own way calls us to good works." I then used what I thought was a clever play on words: "In Hinduism, there exists the 'atman' or 'world soul,' which is the beginning of all souls; in science, the 'atom' sits at life's beginning; in Christianity, we all come from 'Adam.' So it does not matter whether we refer to atman, atom or Adam; whether we are Christian or followers of Krishna—they all even sound the same."

I spoke confidently. Not only had my words silenced these new believers, but I also bewildered them. I "counter-witnessed" and won. The result was that their faith was shaken while my philosophy remained secure. The discussion was over, and with an awkward silence filling the room, I turned and scooted my chair back to its spot at the head of the table. There, resting on the place setting, was a large, "red-letter" Bible that someone had left open to the eighteenth chapter of the book of Matthew.

You should understand that, along with the "holy books" I read from other religions, I also esteemed the Bible. It was a book through which God spoke. Now something strange began happening to me. I was not reading this Bible on the table; it was "reading" me. My attention had been captured by the bloodred words of the sixth verse:

> Whoever causes one of these little ones who believe in Me to stumble, it would be better for him to have a heavy millstone hung around his neck, and to be drowned in the depth of the sea.
>
> Matthew 18:6

Up to that moment, I had been thinking fairly well of myself. In fact, I thought I had just "enlightened" three naive young Christians, helping them not to be so narrow-minded. Suddenly the words of this verse, like lightning, bolted into my eyes and shot straight into the darkness of my heart. Throughout my entire being I was instantly aware that the God of these Christians was angry with me. I had just done what this verse warned against: I had caused His little ones to stumble!

All my philosophers, those supposedly great sages whose books I devoured, had left their ideas to mankind and then departed; *but Jesus Christ was actually with these young Christians!* He was not a mere religion. He was their living Shepherd and capable Savior—and He was protecting them from me!

My *invisible friend* was suddenly no longer friendly! He became aggressively hostile. The impact of His anger was like a punch to my chest. It knocked the breath from my lungs. The color drained from my face. My palms began to sweat.

I felt physically wounded!

I might have just won the debate, but I was rapidly, unconditionally, losing the war. I could not talk, except to manage a frail "I'm sorry" as I stumbled toward the bathroom, which was the only place in the crowded farmhouse where I could be alone.

"Lord, please forgive me. I will never do that again," I said repeatedly as I sat trembling on the bathroom floor. Then I had a revelation: Just as the ancient sages trained and mentored their followers, since Jesus Christ was truly alive, perhaps He would accept me as His disciple. Obviously, though invisible, He had no problem communicating with me! In His mercy, the Lord was building a bridge into my thought processes so He could personally free me from my deception.

I still did not "officially" become a Christian—that would happen two days later on Thanksgiving night. But now, in a frightening way, I knew Jesus was real. I also knew, eternally and indelibly, that the way to quickly rouse His anger was to cause a new believer to stumble.

The Holy Fear of God

We have an erroneous idea that God is a little like Santa Claus: always jovial, kind and busy working on a new present for us. But the Almighty is not a harmless Santa Claus. In fact, there are certain things He actually abhors—such things that compel Him to wrath.

What kind of life do you think awaits the man who is doing what God hates? The book of Proverbs lists seven attitudes that will surely and quickly invoke God's wrath. The worst thing He hates He mentions last:

> There are six things which the LORD hates, yes, seven which are an abomination to Him: haughty eyes, a lying tongue, and hands that shed innocent blood, a heart that devises wicked plans, feet that run rapidly to evil, a false witness who utters lies, and one who spreads strife among brothers.
>
> Proverbs 6:16–19

Each of these sins manifests itself in varying degrees during a church split, the worst offense being to spread strife among brothers. God hates this for many reasons, but the most terrible thing it does is cause little ones to stumble.

If we are involved in spreading strife, we are awakening God's wrath. You see, a church is not a "religious museum" where ancient artifacts are revered; it is a community united by a common relationship with Christ and through Christ, and thereby its members are united with one another. From heaven's view, God dwells in the harmony of our common relationship with Him.

God defines eternal life by the condition of our relationships. Yet in a church split, relationships are brutalized and many people stumble. Old friends become new enemies. People who once prayed for each other now prey on each other. Worse, new believers stumble badly, wondering how

mature, spiritual leaders could divide over such inconse-
quential issues usually accompanying church divisions.
Meanwhile, because of such pettiness, "pre-believers,"
those close to coming to Christ, recognize this cannot pos-
sibly be right, and they walk away from God.

Instead of rivers of living water flowing from the in-
nermost being of church fellowship, a deep, sickening feeling churns in the pit of every stomach. The whole church
feels it. This is so serious, so opposite the essence of God's
Kingdom. Jesus tells us that if we are at the altar and there
remember someone has something against us, we are commanded to leave our offering and be reconciled with our
brother (see Matthew 5:23–24). He is saying, in effect, "Your
religious church service is not as important to Me as your
relationship with your estranged brother."

Let Us Win Souls, Not Offend Them!

Jesus said, "Woe to that man through whom the stumbling block comes!" (Matthew 18:7). Dear ones, listen: If
you are following a man willing to split a church to fulfill
a ministry call, beware. How can one who willingly tears
apart relationships be genuinely concerned about relationships? How can anyone who is willing to cause little ones
to stumble be walking toward the blessing and approval
of Jesus Christ?

I have told you the story of how I came to Christ and the
warning the Lord gave me. Beloved friend, if you desire to
start a church, find ways that do not divide your present
church or cause people to stumble. God has protocols that
must be followed. If what we are planning has caused division, and children and new believers are stumbling, then
we are absolutely going in the wrong direction.

Leaders, in order to safeguard our churches from division, we must have a church growth strategy that creates

positive, redemptive opportunities for people to be released in ministry functions. This may be as simple as a recommended Bible college or as sophisticated as a broad church planting strategy. Let us develop clear, positive alternatives so church splits do not become options. While we must protect the flock, let us not become possessive. God gives us authority to spiritually liberate His people and equip them for ministry. Let's do our part to find ways to train and release maturing Christians.

I have never recovered from that first frightening encounter with God. It abides as a living, holy fear within me. I am concerned for new believers. I know that the Lord Himself will personally turn hostile for the sake of His sheep, and I cannot bear the thought of rousing God's anger against me. So in defense of the Lord's people and in service to the Lord's heart, I repeat to you the words of the Lord Jesus Christ:

Whoever causes one of these little ones who believe in Me to stumble, it would be better for him to have a heavy millstone hung around his neck, and to be drowned in the depth of the sea.

Matthew 18:6

Lord Jesus, forgive me for thinking my needs were more important than Yours and the needs of children. Master, You taught that children are the most important people in Your Kingdom. Father, forgive me for causing them to stumble. In Jesus' name. Amen.

Part 2

How Strife
Begins

For lack of wood the fire goes out,
and where there is no whisperer,
contention quiets down.
Like charcoal to hot embers
and wood to fire,
so is a contentious man
to kindle strife.

Proverbs 26:20–21

Lucifer's Nature: Ambition

No virtue manifests in our lives without Satan awakening a corresponding vice: Traveling with obedience is pride, and just behind faith walks presumption. Yes, and walking in the shadow of godly vision, ambition follows.

There are perhaps many sources of strife that lead to divisions and splits, but none are more subtle or powerful than religious ambition. This is especially so when a subordinate leader begins to imagine God has called him to take the place of a senior leader or department head.

This powerful source of strife certainly was behind the first great division. Through the voice of the Babylonian king mentioned in Isaiah 14 (actually identified as "Lucifer" in the King James Bible), the Holy Spirit gives us insight into the motive of Lucifer's rebellion against divine authority: selfish ambition. Listen to the edict of God against the unholy objectives of the prince of darkness:

How you are fallen from heaven, O Lucifer, son of the morning! How you are cut down to the ground, you who weakened the nations! For you have said in your heart: "I will ascend into heaven, I will exalt my throne above the stars of God; I will also sit on the mount of the congregation on the farthest sides of the north; I will ascend above the heights of the clouds, I will be like the Most High."

Isaiah 14:12–14, NKJV

A number of Bible commentators agree that this quote, though ascribed to a man, actually embodies Lucifer's unrestrained lust for preeminence and position. Five times the focus of Lucifer's pride speaks through the king's great ambition: "I will." The final time he states plainly his unholy quest to supplant God as the Supreme Being worshiped on planet earth.

Lucifer not only desires to be like God, but he also seeks to "ascend into heaven" and establish his throne above the stars of God, which is where the Almighty sits! The Revelation of John confirms this goal repeatedly throughout the book: Satan seeks to be worshiped. He seeks the place of God in heaven, and he seeks the place of God in us.

This is vital for our discernment: *Satan is primarily a religious spirit.* He does not want to destroy the world; he wants to rule it. He led a third of the angels against God's authority in heaven, and he manipulates religious ambition in subordinate leaders to usurp God's delegated authority in His Church on earth.

Of course, Lucifer's involvement in the religion of man is widespread and multifaceted, but nothing he does is more subtle or diabolical than when he deceives good Christians and causes them to turn against their own church leaders. Astutely, Jesus warned that a "house divided against itself will not stand" (Matthew 12:25).

Listen well: It is right to aspire to the office of an overseer; it is wrong to be ambitious for the office of *your* overseer. It is honorable to desire to serve a church as shepherd; it is hellish to engender discontent against the leader of your current church so you can take his place.

Because a subordinate leader cannot simply take the place of the senior leader through physical force, he must work covertly. He has to make himself appear righteous and find ways to make the senior leader appear unrighteous, or at least not as righteous or wise as the subordinate postures himself to be. The one in rebellion always has an issue. There is always something not right—and if he were in charge, he would do all things better. Reasonable communication or compromise on problems that are not serious sin issues will never remedy the conflict because the subordinate does not want compromise; he desires control. As Lucifer seeks to take the place of God, so the subordinate covets the pastor's position.

Whenever one seeks to take the place of another whom God has placed in authority, he is conforming himself to the image of Lucifer, not Christ.

Godly Vision, Fleshly Motives

The deception surrounding ambition is especially powerful when someone actually has a vision from God but seeks to fulfill it in the flesh. Early in my spiritual journey, the Lord gave me a vision about my future. It was an exciting promise, alive with the glory and power of God, bursting with hope to reach nations for Christ. But while the vision focused me on the presence of the Lord, it came without any specifics as to when or how it would be fulfilled.

In those days I thought the Lord's promise was the same as His command—something I had to fulfill in whatever way I could. Because of my spiritual immaturity, I could find no reason why the Lord's promise should not be fulfilled quickly. (When one is immature, he does not realize he is immature, because he is immature.)

According to my imagination, it would be easy for God to fulfill His promise, and I had a preponderance of ideas to help Him. Young as I was spiritually, I was simply unfamiliar with the Holy Spirit's work of preparation: the call to die to self, the seasons of learning patience and maintaining vision through testing—all of which needed to occur before the vision from the Almighty would draw near to fulfillment.

A true word from God will test you before it fulfills you. Consider Joseph. The Scripture says, "Until the time that his word came to pass, the word of the LORD tested him" (Psalm 105:19). The longer my spiritual fulfillment delayed, the more my character was being forced to change. With great passion I wanted my destiny to unfold; I just did not want God's discipline. With unrelenting hope, I desired the crown God set before me; I just did not see the cross that stood between the Father's initial promise and my spiritual fulfillment.

Thankfully, even though in my earlier years I wrestled with my own ambitions of spiritual fulfillment and even made a few mistakes, I never sought the place of another leader. I learned to trust in the Lord and do right. I saw that fretting over what was wrong in those around me led only to evildoing. In His great patience, the Lord taught me to delight myself in Him. I know if a certain promotion is truly His will for me, then He will open the door at the proper time.

Ambition

I have come to believe that it is probably impossible to gain spiritual advancement without ambition rising within us. I do not even think ambition, in and of itself, is blatantly wrong as long as zeal is guarded by humility and submission. To have ambition yet be able to wait, trust God, and put others first means the Holy Spirit rules our lives and thus transforms ambition into patient obedience. It is when ambition and pride unite that we become spiritually dangerous.

But even if our motives are not perfect, we need to persist with our destinies. We must not become so introspective that we stop walking forward. Many times, especially in our early years, we must persevere in spite of our pride and fleshly motives. We must ask God to correct us as we move forward; we must not be afraid to take faith, and step out. Be aware, however, of those times when zeal can create strife and confusion. For when we are causing strife, we are moving away from our destiny, not toward it.

Ambition might arise as a consequence of faith, but it is not faith. Ambition is the attempt of the flesh to fulfill the promise of the Spirit. In my inner person I considered my ambition to be a virtue; I was actually proud of it. Abraham, too, showed ambition when, in his impatience, he lay with Hagar to produce Ishmael. Ultimately the Lord said of Ishmael, "He will be a wild donkey of a man, his hand will be against everyone, and everyone's hand will be against him" (Genesis 16:12). In other words, he would be a constant source of strife. Ambition, when driving us to move ahead of the Lord's timing, will almost always produce strife in those around us.

True faith, however, rests in God's integrity and faithfulness. A person of faith can entrust his calling and gifts to the timing and wisdom of God. Thus, true faith rests in God, even when what is promised is not yet seen. It does not strive; it trusts. Abraham's faith outgrew his ambition because he learned to trust that the Lord was faithful (see Hebrews 10:23). He became "fully assured that what God had promised, He was able also to perform" (Romans 4:21).

The overly ambitious soul, however, fails to trust God for the timing and opening of appropriate doors; it spawns impatience and strives to fulfill its own destiny. Ambition tries to create doors where none exist.

The Bible tells us plainly that none of those whom God used were able to avoid an extended time of preparation. God's call and His timing are the work of His hands. Our task is to remain faithful to the place He has put us and to maintain integrity in support of others.

Unrestrained ambition creates strife, in part because it is rooted in fear. This fear brings striving and jealousy into the Christian soul, especially as others occupy positions we deem necessary for our fulfillment. Because we do not truly know the Lord in the way of patience and trust, the voice we most often obey is not God's; rather, it is the urgency of our own ambition.

Consequently James tells us, "Where jealousy and selfish ambition exist," there will inevitably emerge "disorder and every evil thing" (James 3:16). Disorder comes as people violate proper protocols for spiritual advancement and begin to criticize those in positions over or alongside them. Disorder opens the door for "every evil thing" to enter, as the pastor's attention is drawn away from his God-appointed responsibilities and is given instead to lengthy—and usually fruitless—meetings trying to remedy strife.

Ambition is obsessed with fulfillment. When rebuked, though it puts on the face of the penitent, it grows angrier because of the new delay. There is only one remedy for religious ambition: It must die.

The Path to Leadership

If you are a subordinate leader and desire your own church, do not find fault with your current leader as a means of seeking advancement. The answer to your success is unveiled in Psalm 37. Here David revealed the attitude that ultimately promoted him to kingship. Remember: David was submitted to King Saul, an unjust king driven by fits of madness. Still, David wrote,

> Trust in the LORD and do good; dwell in the land and cultivate faithfulness. Delight yourself in the LORD; and He will give you the desires of your heart. Commit your way to the LORD, trust also in Him, and He will do it. He will bring forth your righteousness as the light and your judgment as the noonday. Rest in the LORD and wait patiently for Him; do not fret because of him who prospers in his way, because of the man who carries out wicked schemes. Cease from anger and forsake wrath; do not fret; it leads only to evildoing.
>
> Psalm 37:3–8

David has outlined for us the true path to leadership. Let us, therefore, cease from anger and forsake wrath. Let us delight ourselves in the Lord, and He will give us the desires of our hearts at the proper time.

> *Lord Jesus, forgive me for my selfish motives and unbroken will. I confess there have been times when my pride and ambition have generated strife. I have been so blind to this. Help me to serve You with my whole heart and let You promote me at the proper time. For Your glory I pray. Amen.*

Three Spiritual Enemies of Unity

> It is important to realize that, while we are dealing with the weakness of flesh and blood, our true fight is not against people; it is against "spiritual forces of wickedness" (Ephesians 6:12).

Just as we discussed in chapter 2 that the issue is not the issue, so the apparent enemy is not the real enemy. We are fighting not people but the spirits that manipulate immature or sinful attitudes of heart in people. These spirits seek to gain access to our churches and families; they must be discerned. Religious ambition in the human heart is just the entry point for the enemies we are truly fighting: the spirits of division and strife.

The nature and goal of these spirits are the same: to inspire someone to seek in an ungodly way another person's position of authority, thus causing division. This is the ancient battle transported to modern times with flesh and blood role players. Recall Jude's warning:

> And angels who did not keep their own domain, but abandoned their proper abode, He has kept in eternal bonds under darkness for the judgment of the great day.
>
> Jude 1:6

When we unethically abandon our "proper abode" and seek the role of another, we embrace the very sin Lucifer and his angels committed. Just as their sin led to hell, so their manipulation of earthly ambitions extends hell into the lives of men and women on earth.

While the spirits of division and strife share the same goal of creating division, their approaches to separating people are unique. The Old Testament provides three examples of individuals who usurped authority and divided the people of God: Korah, Absalom and Jezebel. Although these individuals were real people with historic lives, for the sake of classification we will assign their names to the spirits that manipulated them. When we discuss these enemies, we are looking through the human personality at the spirit that seeks to find modern counterparts and again bring strife among God's people.

Korah: The Leader Who Wants It All

The New Testament writer Jude mentions specifically the "rebellion of Korah" (Jude 1:11). Korah was a leader in ancient Israel; he was equal to Aaron in authority and was a cousin to both Moses and Aaron. Through his influence he was able to seduce 250 of Israel's princes to join him in a rebellion against Moses.

The worst divisions among God's people are those led by subordinate leaders who have acquired a large following. *Matthew Henry's Commentary* says of Korah and the other leaders in rebellion: "Note, the pride, ambition and emulation of great men have always been the occasion of a great deal of mischief both in churches and states. . . . The fame and renown they had did not content them; they were high, but would be higher, and thus the famous men became infamous." Although Matthew Henry is speaking of Korah, clearly he could be describing Lucifer himself or any subordinate leader who has tasted success, is discontent he does not have more power and envies those above him.

Listen to Korah's accusation against Moses and Aaron: "You take too much upon yourselves. . . . Why then do you exalt yourselves above the assembly of the LORD?" (Numbers 16:3, NKJV). While it is Korah who is in rebellion, he charges that *Moses* is rebelling against God and is domineering in his leadership. It is Korah who is seeking to exalt himself, yet he accuses Moses and Aaron of exalting themselves "above the assembly."

As a means of spiritual discernment, listen carefully to the one who accuses your pastoral leadership. Even before you examine your pastor, examine his accuser. You will often see in him the very flaws he says are in the pastor.

As a further argument, Korah states, "All [Israel] is holy . . . and the Lord is among them" (NKJV). The implication is that Korah is actually the one most concerned for the people—that Moses' task is complete and it is time for new leadership to be appointed.

Of course, at this time all Israel was not holy, nor was the assignment of Moses complete. But Korah said these things to reinforce the accusation that Moses was a domineering personality who was seeking primarily to maintain control of Israel.

Friends, at times a senior leader truly may be overly controlling, and we will discuss that soon. But at other times our wrong attitudes toward authority cause us to misjudge a leader as "controlling" when he is, in fact, simply fulfilling his God-given spiritual responsibility. God appointed Moses as Israel's leader. God chose him on the basis of his meekness—a trait that was little esteemed by those who sought to remove him from leadership. Remember: To usurp the authority God has installed is to sin against the Lord Himself.

Moses responded to Korah:

> "Hear now, you sons of Levi, is it not enough for you that the God of Israel has separated you from the rest of the congregation of Israel, to bring you near to Himself, to do the service of the tabernacle of the LORD, and to stand before the congregation to minister to them; and that He has brought you near, Korah, and all your brothers, sons of Levi, with you? And are you seeking for the priesthood also?"
>
> Numbers 16:8–10

Moses exposes the sins of envy and ambition in Korah's heart. He asks, "Is it not enough for you" that you already have a position set apart to God? Ambition walks upon two legs: envy and pride. Whenever we covet the position God has assigned to another, we attract the Lord's anger to ourselves. Indeed, the story of Korah's rebellion concludes with the ground swallowing Korah and those in rebellion with him.

It is important to note that both Korah and Jethro, Moses' father-in-law, approached Moses with a similar statement. Korah was confrontational and filled with ambition and rebellion; Jethro was humble and filled with concern. When Jethro saw all Moses was doing he said, "What is this thing that you are doing for the people? Why do you alone sit as judge and all the people stand about you from morning until evening?" (Exodus 18:14).

To express concern to a leader in a humble manner is an asset to any church; to confront the leader out of pride and ambition, as did Korah, is to expose one's self to the wrath of God. Korah's confrontation and rebellion led to death, but under Jethro's counsel Israel prospered. Never be afraid to submit observations to leaders. Give advice, but then let them administrate as they see fit.

An interesting side note is that the sons of Korah did not die in their father's rebellion. They chose instead to be submissive to Moses and Aaron. In time the sons of Korah held a place of great honor in David's day, actually writing a number of the Psalms, which we study today as sacred Scriptures.

To be free from the influences of the Korah spirit, we must be content to wholeheartedly serve God where He has currently placed us. A time may come when a new order or new assignment comes from the Holy Spirit, but until then the Lord will not require us to challenge the authority of those over us or divide the church in order to fulfill our religious ambitions.

The Absalom Spirit

Nelson's Bible Dictionary states, "Absalom was the third son by Maacah, the daughter of the king of Geshur (2 Samuel 3:3; 1 Chronicles 3:2). Of royal descent on both sides, Absalom was a potential heir to the throne. Attractive in appearance and charming in manners, he was also a popular prince with the people and a favorite of his father."

Although a favorite of his father and the people, Absalom suffered the injustice of his half sister's rape by Amnon, another of David's sons. In retaliation, Absalom had Amnon murdered by his servants. Fearing the wrath of his father for the murder of Amnon, he fled to Geshur, where he lived in exile for three years. Finally, under pressure from his leaders, David reluctantly sent for Absalom but shunned him when he returned. The long delay and his father's indifference produced bitterness in Absalom toward the king, which ripened into a plan to steal his father's throne:

> Absalom used to rise early and stand beside the way to the gate; and when any man had a suit to come to the king for judgment, Absalom would call to him and say, "From what city are you?" And he would say, "Your servant is from one of the tribes of Israel." Then Absalom would say to him, "See, your claims are good and right, but no man listens to you on the part of the king." Moreover, Absalom would say, "Oh that one would appoint me judge in the land, then every man who has any suit or cause could come to me and I would give him justice." And when a man came near to prostrate himself before him, he would put out his hand and take hold of him and kiss him. In this manner Absalom dealt with all Israel who came to the king for judgment; so Absalom stole away the hearts of the men of Israel.
>
> 2 Samuel 15:2–6

Just as Lucifer sought the place of God and Korah sought the place of Moses, so Absalom coveted the kingship of his father, David. At first, however, Absalom was not openly confrontational and did not seek to challenge the king's authority. Rather, Absalom used his charm and subtle criticisms of the king to steal away the hearts of men. Absalom found fault with David and engendered grumbling in the people of Israel, while winning the hearts of the people with flattery and charm.

The New Testament writer Jude again gives us an insight into this manipulating spirit as it manifests today through people:

> These are grumblers, finding fault, following after their own lusts; they speak arrogantly, flattering people for the sake of gaining an advantage. . . . These are the ones who cause divisions, worldly-minded, devoid of the Spirit.
>
> Jude 1:16, 19

"These are the ones who cause divisions." The plan of the Absalom spirit is simple: Grumble about the way things are not getting done, find fault with the leader and arrogantly project the image that, if you were in charge, all would be well. Then, to capture the hearts of the people, flatter them and bring them into your camp. Paul also warned about those whom he called "savage wolves," who "will arise, speaking perverse things, to draw away the disciples after them" (Acts 20:29, 30).

To speak "perverse things" means to twist or distort the truth. Beware when someone comes along complaining about the way things are done, speaking evil of the church leader and promoting himself as an answer to these problems. You are probably listening to a wolf in the flock of God. Yet even in this situation, speak with this person directly and expose his error. Perhaps the Lord will change his heart.

What if the suspicions raised against the senior leader seem to be true? Matthew 18:15–17 outlines the appropriate way to handle this situation. Before you talk to anyone in the congregation, go to the leader himself. Go in meekness, entreating him "as a father" (1 Timothy 5:1). Hear his side. If he is guilty of serious sin and remains unrepentant, bring with you two or three others. If he continues in sin, public exposure of his error is the final remedy. But before you expose it, your group should approach other church leaders in the city or the denomination's district supervisor. Let them administrate the proper discipline.

At the same time, you must be certain that he is in serious sin. It is not enough to just "sense" that there is "something wrong under the surface." You must have facts. If his primary "sin" is that he does not feel comfortable going along with the current trend in American Christianity, this is not sin. If you yourself feel you must see certain spiritual manifestations in church, go somewhere where the things you seek are occurring. But do not divide your church or speak things to draw disciples after yourself. If you dream of being the leader of the church and are using spiritual phenomena to justify building a constituency, you are walking in the footsteps of Absalom, not Christ.

To free yourself from the influences of the Absalom spirit, repent of pride and refrain from using flattery to gain an advantage among the people. Instead of manipulating the unmet needs of the church to gain a following, submit yourself and your talents to the church leaders. Ask them how you can help. Do not exploit the needs; help meet them. And when you have been used by the Lord, point people to Christ, securing them in the care of the church leaders.

(For further insight on the nature of Absalom, read *A Tale of Three Kings* by Gene Edwards.)

The Jezebel Spirit

In the Old Testament, Jezebel was a queen who fought against authority, whether that authority was resident in the spiritual leaders (the prophets) or the secular leader (the king). In the New Testament, Jesus mentions this spirit again, this time manifest as a prophetess in the church in Thyatira. In both settings this spirit desires to neutralize authority and take control over other people in the church and family.

When the Jezebel spirit attacks church leadership, its ultimate purpose is to disable the spiritual authority of pastoral leadership. The attack may come in the form of sexual temptation, confusion or prophetic manipulation, but its ultimate aim is to supplant the authority in the church. The Jezebel spirit seeks to divide, diminish and then displace the spiritual authority God has given church leaders. Thus, Jesus promised that the church that overcomes Jezebel would be granted "authority over the nations" (Revelation 2:26).

While Korah and Absalom use issues that most often affect men, Jezebel targets women. In the New Testament, Jesus Himself referred to Jezebel as a "woman . . . who calls herself a prophetess" (Revelation 2:20). Catch this phrase: she "calls herself." In other words, she is self-appointed and submitted to no one. She uses her prophetic insights and sensitivities to draw a following to herself, again dividing the church from its true base of authority.

If you are a woman who has a propensity to gain control in relationships, the antidote for this influence is true humility. Let the Lord promote you. Stay submissive. Jezebel's quest for control masks a deeper need she has concerning fear. She was probably abused and is afraid of being abused again, so she seeks to control her world using whatever means available. To be healed from the influence of Jezebel, whether it attaches itself to a woman or a man, one must truly learn to trust God.

A Word about Intercessors

Because the Jezebel spirit wars against authority in the church, it seeks to put wedges of division between a pastor and the church intercessors. To counter this potential division, the senior leader must appreciate, communicate with and support his intercessors and esteem their contribution, and the intercessors should set their prayer focus to seek the spiritual fulfillment of their pastor's vision.

Without pastors leading in godly authority, a church simply cannot function: confusion, ambition and chaos reign. True spiritual authority is a source of protection; it is a living shelter that covers and nurtures a home or church. Satan seeks to neutralize the leader in that Christian setting, for if he can strike the shepherd, then he can scatter the sheep.

And we need intercessors, for prayer is the frontier of transformation. Without intercessors the church would not move forward. The senior leader may draw his vision for the church directly from the Lord or indirectly from his staff. He may find direction from Christian authors, denominational leadership, or some combination of the above. Not the least of his resources, however, are the church intercessors. I personally have been rescued and protected by the faithfulness of humble intercessors who stand in the gap before God on my behalf.

When an intercessor assumes, however, that his or her "prophetic witness" is the guiding light of the church, or when he or she stands apart from the church leadership and promotes a different vision than what the leadership presents, that intercessor introduces strife and confusion to God's people. This is a sign that the spirit of Jezebel may be trying to divide that church.

In such situations, those who present a vision different from the pastor's are usually presenting something that seems godly and reasonable, so the confusion spreads. But the unbending demand that a leader conform to a prophetic witness or the urgency of its timing is where the enemy gains access and causes division. Intercessors must accept that God has given the church leadership the responsibility to guide the church. If God has given you a prophetic witness, then submit your perceptions and spiritual aspirations to the church leaders and trust God to bring it to pass, if He so chooses, in its proper time. If any change of direction is to come, it should come through the administration of church leadership.

Intercessors, make your stand to defend the word spoken from the pulpit by the pastor. If his or her teaching is boring and unimaginative, all the more reason to pray. Take his or her sermon and focus your prayer on that theme during the coming week. There is nothing more powerful than when the teaching in a church and the intercession of that church are in agreement (see Zechariah 12:10; 1 Peter 4:11).

No wonder Jezebel seeks to divide the intercessors from the leaders. When intercessors pray what the pastor preaches, the union of the Spirit and the Word releases the creative power of heaven itself.

> *Lord, help me to see and understand my role in Your Kingdom. Master, grant me the meekness of the Holy Spirit, that I might serve without ambition, encourage without manipulation and intercede without trying to control. Lord, help me to walk in discernment. Free me from any influence other than the ministry of the Holy Spirit Himself. In Jesus' name. Amen.*

One of You Is a Gossip

A perverse man spreads strife, and a slanderer separates intimate friends.

Proverbs 16:28

Jesus made a remarkable statement concerning Judas: "'Did I Myself not choose you, the twelve, and yet one of you is a devil?' Now He meant Judas the son of Simon Iscariot, for he, one of the twelve, was going to betray Him" (John 6:70–71).

To what was Jesus referring when He identified Judas Iscariot as a "devil"? Was He speaking figuratively or factually? Is Jesus saying that a human being could not only have an evil spirit living in his soul, but that a person could actually become a demon?

Some teach that Judas had become so perfectly possessed by Satan that he actually lost his humanity. Before we accept this interpretation, let us remember that after this fallen apostle delivered Jesus up, he felt such remorse for betraying Christ that he committed suicide. Could a demon feel such remorse for sin? I do not think so.

What I believe Jesus is identifying in Judas Iscariot as a "devil" is something that, today, exists unchecked among many Christians: *slander*. In the New Testament, the Greek word *diabolos*, which is translated "devil" in this text, is translated impersonally elsewhere as a "false accuser," "slanderer" or "malicious gossip." In fact, 1 Timothy 3:11 and 2 Timothy 3:3 both translate *diabolos* (*Strong's Exhaustive Concordance of the Bible*, #1228) as "malicious gossip(s)."

In other words, Jesus is not saying "one of you is a devil" in an organic or theological sense, but that one of you is "a slanderer, a malicious gossip." So while the disciples were almost bragging about their loyalty to Christ, Jesus corrected them, in effect saying, "Yes, I chose you, but even among you there is one who is a malicious gossip, whose words will eventually betray Me to My enemies."

Gossip in the Last Days

This problem of gossip in the Church, Paul tells us, will continue right into the end of the age. Listen carefully to what Paul wrote to Timothy about the last days: "Men will be lovers of self, lovers of money, boastful, arrogant, revilers, disobedient to parents, ungrateful, unholy, unloving, irreconcilable, malicious gossips" (2 Timothy 3:2–3), and the list goes on. In the midst of this list of great sins of the apostasy, the apostle includes "malicious gossips." This is the exact same word translated "devil" in John 6:70.

Perhaps you know people who always have something negative to say about others, who always bring negative information about people into their conversations. I pray that the Holy Spirit will reveal to us how "malicious gossip" is kin to the nature of Satan himself!

The Scriptures say that we will be justified or condemned by our words. Yes, our words—even those spoken in secret with a spouse or friend about others—are used by God to measure our obedience to His will. James writes, "If anyone does not stumble in what he says, he is a perfect man" (James 3:2).

Words have power. Scripture reveals that "death and life are in the power of the tongue" (Proverbs 18:21). Our words, expressed as a confession of faith, bring us into salvation; but words without faith can lead us and others with us into destruction and heartache.

James 3:8 warns, "The tongue . . . is a restless evil . . . full of deadly poison." "The tongue," he says, "is a fire, the very world of iniquity" (verse 6). And James reveals a most profound thought: "The tongue . . . sets on fire the course of our life, and is set on fire by hell" (verse 6).

Satan gains access to our world, to destroy all that is good and holy in it, through our tongues. The very course of our life, the direction and quality of our earthly existence, is "set on fire by hell" through the words we speak. If we talk negatively about someone or maliciously gossip, the destructive fire of hell itself is released through our words. Lord, help us to understand the power of our words!

I believe God wants to break the power of gossip and negative speaking from the Church. We may have a perfect analysis of what is wrong and why it is evil, yet if all we do is talk about it, we have yet to disavow our allegiance to hell. God calls us to be a house of prayer *for* all nations—a spiritual community that is mature, fully capable of seeing what is wrong, but positioning itself to release redemption into the world.

If Paul Visited Your Community

Imagine if the apostle Paul came into a typical American city. Do you know what he might say about our divisions? Probably what he told the Corinthians: "I am afraid that perhaps when I come . . . there will be strife, jealousy, angry tempers, disputes, slanders, gossip, arrogance, disturbances" (2 Corinthians 12:20).

Does that remind you of any churches anywhere? Strife? Jealousy? Slander and gossip? How can we approach God with these things existing in us? I believe God desires to give the Church a whole new approach. But we cannot lay hold of the future unless we first let go of the past.

Perhaps you are thinking, "So and so should hear this." Yes, but we must start with ourselves. Pastors must stop talking negatively about people; they need to refrain from "leaking" problems with people into their sermons. Intercessors must stop negative gossip about the people for whom they should be praying. If we discuss what is wrong for ten minutes, let us pray for redemption for twenty.

Judge Not

How do you respond to life's imperfections? Do you gossip? When you hear of someone's failure, are you quick to spread the news? If Jesus was looking at the Christians with whom you fellowship, would He say to you what He spoke to His early apostles, that "one of you is a malicious gossip?"

Even if you are not a gossip or slanderer, you must be careful to avoid "fellowship" with gossips. Criticisms incubate. Paul warned that "a little leaven leavens the whole lump" (1 Corinthians 5:6). If we walk with the wise, we will become wise, but if we open our hearts to the cynical and critical, then we become like them. That is why Jesus said we were to "take heed" to what we hear. For whatever we intently focus upon, we absorb in abundance (see Mark 4:24).

Thus, we must not even listen to gossip. When God shows us what is wrong in life, it is so we can pray for redemption, not spread the bad news all over town. Prayer has a positive focus. People with Christ's love have a spiritual vision that causes them to see beyond the imperfections and limitations of the present world into the potential awaiting in the future—and they pray until what they see comes to pass.

Remember: None of us stands perfectly upright. Every time we judge someone, we position ourselves to be judged as well. Indeed, we each continually lean in the direction of our weakness. Only by the grace of God are we kept from falling. The moment we begin to self-righteously judge or gossip about another for their failings, we lean a little closer toward our own fall.

Our actions and words should be motivated by mercy. If we must discuss the situation or individual, let us harbor no malice or ill will. Let redemption be our guide, not revenge. Let us keep ourselves from becoming those who betray the working of Christ on earth. Let us keep ourselves from the realm of the malicious gossip.

> *Lord, purify my lips with fire from Your*
> *holy altar. Father, forgive me for my words*
> *that have not always been redemptive. Lord,*
> *deliver the Church from the realm of spreading*
> *gossip to the work of spreading grace. Help us*
> *to be a house of prayer. In Jesus' name. Amen.*

Part 3

Healing the
Wounded
Church

I will extol You, O LORD,
for You have lifted me up,
and have not let my enemies
rejoice over me.
O LORD my God,
I cried to You for help,
and You healed me.

Psalm 30:1–2

When a Leader Sins

Not many things are more devastating than when someone in authority—someone whom we trust—betrays our trust and chooses sin. Unless we deal with the effect of a leader's sin, it will always be a source of oppression to us.

Sometimes the motivating force behind a church split has to do with the sins of church leadership. I am not referring to minor offenses or flaws but to sins that are either sexual in nature or a violation of community laws that could lead to incarceration.

Zechariah warns, "Strike the Shepherd that the sheep may be scattered; and I will turn My hand against the little ones" (Zechariah 13:7). This Scripture refers, of course, to Jesus Christ. He did not sin but was slandered as though He had sinned. Either way, the effect was the same: a scattering of the little ones.

Satan knows that when the shepherd of a flock is struck, "little ones" are scattered. Thus, there will almost always be more spiritual warfare against a leader than that which typically comes against the church in general. Indeed, much of the warfare against a church is a direct result of the battle against its leader or leadership.

Sometimes, however, leaders do fall. Men and women alike can fail to gauge the cunning of the enemy and become entrapped in serious sin. When such sin is finally exposed, it has a devastating effect upon a church—so much so that people leave en masse. This kind of split is not caused by the ambition of those who leave but by the failing of one in leadership. For both those who leave and those who remain, a cleansing is necessary in order to guide the sheep back into the blessedness of God's presence.

The Effects of a Leader's Sin

When church leaders serve the living Christ in love, aggressive faith and prayerful humility, the people who dwell in that atmosphere become rich in the presence of God. Conversely, when leaders blatantly sin or are led into deception, the heartache of their downfall is absorbed into the spirits of those in their care.

This precept—that a leader's sin carries negative consequences—is not something with which we are unfamiliar. Do you remember what you felt when you heard of the sins of Bill Clinton, our former president? Or when Jimmy Swaggart fell? Or consider the distress that crushes a family when a parent falls into serious iniquity. Unless it is remedied, the impact of these events is similar to that of a curse upon one's life.

A biblical example is when David ordered Joab, a general, to take a census of Israel. Joab begged the king, "Why does my lord want to do this? Why should he bring guilt on Israel?" (1 Chronicles 21:3, NIV). David's sin of putting his trust in numbers brought "guilt on Israel" and a plague struck them, killing thousands. And remember the dread proclamation of Jeremiah concerning the destruction of Jerusalem by the Babylonians: "The adversary and the enemy could enter the gates of Jerusalem. Because of the sins of her prophets and the iniquities of her priests" (Lamentations 4:12–13).

The godly example and care of true spiritual leaders, while imperfect, still creates a living shelter for the people they serve. When leaders vacate their post through serious sin, however, spiritual enemies gain access to the church that they would not otherwise have. Instead of blessedness, oppression fills the spiritual realm of that church.

Facing the Effects of a Leader's Sin

While we may be tempted simply to ignore a leader's sin or pretend it has not affected us, the Lord reveals in the Scriptures that He wants us to face the effects of the leader's sin and deal with its subsequent effect upon His people. In the book of Leviticus the Lord says, "If the anointed priest sins so as to bring guilt on the people, then let him offer to the LORD a bull without defect as a sin offering" (Leviticus 4:3).

"Guilt" in this context is not a direct result of the people's sin. It is, rather, the collective effect of what the leader's sin created within them: fear, shame, heartache, confusion and anger. The "guilt on the people" does not mean that they have sinned but that the effect of their leader's sin has oppressed the congregation, positioning them in an "unblessable state of being."

This unblessed state—be it anger, cynicism or confusion, as understandable as these responses may seem—is now a "guilt on the people." To return to the state of blessedness, the people must journey away from their reaction, which needs to be openly acknowledged and atoned for.

Let Christ Cleanse and Heal

As much as they may wish it were otherwise, a wounded church often carries a discernible cloud of heaviness. For years the influence of the wounding surfaces in mistrust of all leaders. Attitudes of cynicism or fearful anticipations become part of the normal congregational thought-life. Worse, their shared, unremedied pain becomes a beehive of demonic exploitation, where human attitudes of anger and confusion leave the church vulnerable to manipulation by the enemy.

Referring to the effects, or the dwelling place, of unresolved sin, the Amplified Bible gives us an insight into this demonic infestation. It reads, "The shades of the dead are there [specters haunting the scene of past transgressions]" (Proverbs 9:18, AMP).

"Specters haunting the scene of past transgressions." This Scripture tells us that the disappointment and heartache caused by a leader's sin provide the means for demons to "haunt" the church body—if we do not find a way to redeem the failure in Christ. In other words, human reactions and unresolved memories from the past can become a magnet for ongoing warfare. To move into a blessed future, we must be cleansed of the unredeemed past.

What is especially unfortunate is that the unredeemed past can be transferred to new members who join a wounded church, even though those individuals were not partakers of the original wounding. New believers come to churches where mistrust of leadership has residence. Soon, through the osmosis of human relationships, the same fears, mistrust and suspicions that were resident in the older members begin to surface in the life of the new ones.

Simply replacing pastors does not bring healing. What needs replacing is the cloud of heaviness that remains in that church. Not only does the fallen leader need forgiveness, cleansing and renewal in Christ, but what was transferred to the people must be cleansed as well.

God Designed Us for Unity

Perhaps we are tempted to think, *So what? Leaders come and go. I walk with God. Their fall does not affect me.* Individually we may indeed be blessed; but we will never know the descent of the Lord's corporate blessing upon a healed, renewed church until we experience cleansing for the consequences of a pastor's sin.

If we fail to deal with the oppression caused by a leader's fall, it is possible that our future relationships with church leaders will be colored with fear and suspicion. The attitude that "leaders come and go" and that one feels he or she is capable of walking alone is itself a form of oppression. We do not have to walk alone. The voice speaking "leaders come and go" is a wounded voice. Remember: There is greater power in unity than in isolation (see Psalm 133). Although we may have to walk alone at times, God designed us to be interconnected members of a Christ-filled people.

Additionally, the Lord promised He will raise up "shepherds over [His people] and they will tend them; and they will not be afraid any longer, nor be terrified, nor will any be missing" (Jeremiah 23:4). Unless we are cleansed of the effect of our negative experience, the filter of our mistrust and our corresponding isolation might disqualify us from recognizing godly leaders when the Lord brings them to us.

You see, there is a corporate blessing coming to the Church that is greater than the individual blessing, for it carries a unique reward to those who overcome offenses and persevere in faith for each other and their leaders. This is the Pentecost anointing that was available to the 120 in the Upper Room, 108 of which had to overcome the failings of the original twelve. Out of the anointing of unity, God touches multitudes, turns cities and empowers His people with the life of heaven.

Carrying Woundedness

You may say, "Ours is a new church; our leaders have not fallen in sin." Locally, your church may be clean. The people in your church, however, did not float from heaven to earth. They were somewhere when national leaders fell—and one does not have to be a church historian to recall how many major spiritual leaders have fallen in recent years. Each time a minister fell, the "mistrust level" toward all church leaders increased. The cumulative effect of moral failure, both on a national and on a local level, has smothered the fire in many Christian hearts. Some of those hearts may be sitting in your church.

If you are a pastor and you are wondering why people do not respond to your teaching as you would hope, it might be they are carrying woundedness from a previous leader. This former leader may be totally unaffiliated with your church, yet their reaction toward him is keeping them guarded and unable to truly hear from you. Among regular church attendees, this woundedness has been translated into a polite, yet numbing, attitude of unbelief and suspicion toward church leaders in general.

Remember: As a pastor or teacher, your goal is not to prepare a sermon but to prepare a people. Thus, it is imperative that you dispel this cloud of mistrust so that people can once again absorb your message and be changed. Do you see this? They may not hear your teaching at the proper response level because they have distanced themselves from the memory of pain. Distance always hinders hearing.

The Cleansing River of Forgiveness

The antidote for a leader's sin in the Old Testament was to "offer to the LORD a bull without defect as a sin offering" (Leviticus 4:3). Of course, we have a Sacrifice for sins greater than the blood of bulls and goats. Yet until we apply Christ's sacrifice to this need, the need remains and continues to negatively affect us. We must, therefore, present ourselves before God for examination. As we yield to His Holy Spirit, one of the great graces He pours upon us is to make all things new.

On a personal level, this renewal work is as effective as our ability to forgive those who have hurt us and let go of the heartache caused by the shortcomings of our leaders. It is a profound opportunity: We can be delivered from becoming hardened in heart. We can look forward to the future, trusting God for ever more wonderful beginnings.

Just as Daniel represented Israel in repentance before God (see Daniel 9), let me personally repent to you on behalf of those church leaders who have fallen or misrepresented Jesus to you. I ask for your forgiveness. Leaders have fallen and caused you distress and heartache; we have burdened you with a yoke that was not the yoke of Christ, but a yoke of oppression. For the sins of all, I ask for your forgiveness.

As God gives you grace, please release that specific man or woman who misused his or her spiritual authority or betrayed the solemn responsibilities entrusted to him or her. Again, I ask you to forgive leaders who have fallen or failed your expectations.

Positioned in Prayer

Knowing that shepherds experience a greater "striking" from the enemy (see Zechariah 13:7), let us also take up our positions to intercede for our leaders. God never intended that congregations would not participate in their leaders' protection, inspiration and well-being. The power and confidence in your church leadership reflects, at least in part, the answer to your prayers. Paul asked for prayer; Jesus asked for prayer; and your pastor needs your prayer as well. Unprayed-for pastors are vulnerable to the battle in unique ways. If you have not stood in intercession for your church leaders, perhaps you are—at least in a small part—a contributor to their stumbling.

Even good leaders fail. Yet God can raise them back up again. In fact, in some ways a fallen but restored leader has a depth of compassion, a "grace understanding," that makes a wonderful shepherd out of him or her. We should not abandon those who have fallen but observe if their brokenness has truly attracted a new grace from God.

Remember Daniel's words, speaking of our very days: "Some of those who have insight will fall, in order to refine, purge and make them pure until the end time; because it is still to come at the appointed time" (Daniel 11:35). Through Daniel the Holy Spirit tells us that certain leaders "will fall," but God will not abandon them. He will instead "refine, purge and make them pure." Fallen leaders are difficult to bear; but if we are part of the process of sorrow, let us also be part of the restoration—together with Christ. Let us forgive our leaders for where they have failed us and in so doing release ourselves from the oppression of the past.

Lord, again, I forgive those leaders whose failings have caused my heart to harden. Lord, grant them—and me—new grace. Grant that we all could know Your awesome power of renewal. Father, I commit to Your hands the cleansing of my soul from the effects of fallen leaders. Restore us all into the power of Your glorious presence. In Jesus' name. Amen.

A Thankful Heart

Let the peace of Christ rule in your hearts, to which indeed you were called in one body; and be thankful.

Colossians 3:15

We can journey through life angry and proud, which manifests in slander and division, or we can become Christians who truly represent the life of Christ. It was specifically in this regard that Paul wrote, "Rejoice always; pray without ceasing; in everything give thanks; for this is God's will for you" (1 Thessalonians 5:16–18).

Joy, prayer and gratitude—not anger, gossip and slander—are "God's will for you." Paul is saying that when you see something wrong in life, do not lose your joy over it. God is with you; His power is in you. You are heaven-bound, so let the world know your faith by your joy. What you cannot remedy immediately, turn over to God in prayer. Do not descend into anger. Rejoice always! Pray without ceasing! This is the positive, healing approach to life that God gives us.

He continues, "In everything give thanks." We must enter the gates of God's presence with thanksgiving. Several years ago someone whom I love very much went through a confusing time. I prayed and prayed but soon became quietly angry at what seemed to me this person's slow progress. After several months I remember praying, "Lord, I do not know why this person has not changed yet, but do something!" Suddenly the presence of the Lord descended into my spirit and my eyes were opened. I saw that God had answered dozens of my prayers for this person! God was working, but because of my anger and lack of thanksgiving I could not perceive the workings of God.

This is why we must remain thankful. Thanksgiving is the language of faith. The moment we spend time thanking the Lord, we begin to see more clearly what He is actually doing. Our eyes open as our hearts open. I have come to realize that the "world of the ungrateful" is a world inhabited by demons.

Listen to what God's Word says:

> For even though they knew God, they did not honor Him as God or give thanks, but they became futile in their speculations, and their foolish heart was darkened. . . . And just as they did not see fit to acknowledge God any longer, God gave them over to a depraved mind, to do those things which are not proper, being filled with all unrighteousness, wickedness, greed, evil; full of envy, murder, strife, deceit, malice; they are gossips [and] slanderers.
>
> Romans 1:21, 28–30

They knew God but did not "honor Him as God or give thanks." As a result God gave them over to a depraved mind. Think of it: We either have a mind that honors and thanks God or we wind up with a depraved mind, full of envy, strife, gossip and slander. The world of the ungrateful spirals ever downward until they become "futile in their speculations" and their hearts are "darkened." Theirs is a world in darkness. Let me say it again: If we are not attaining a thankful spirit, then we are slipping toward a depraved mind.

This spirit of ingratitude, of discontent and grumbling, has penetrated many throughout the Body of Christ. Gossip is so prevalent in the Church today that it has been elevated to the status of tradition.

It is my passionate, focused desire to see every one of us genuinely delivered from the deception of discontent. My prayer is that each of us will rediscover the good life God has waiting for us. If we have come to Christ, then we have received every blessing in the heavenly places (see Ephesians 1:3). But the capacity to actually *receive* God's blessings is only as functional as our ability to be truly grateful for them. Gratitude is the gateway through which God's blessings enter our lives.

So if you are one who has a propensity toward gossip, repent. Renounce speaking evil of others. Do you want to love life and see good days? Keep your tongue from speaking evil and your lips from uttering deceit (see Psalm 34:13). Become an intercessor. If you are in need of forgiveness for gossip, for backbiting, for slander or for ungratefulness, this is the time to ask for it and to seek in its place a thankful heart.

Lord Jesus, forgive me for murmuring and complaining. When I consider that You died for my sins, that You have given me all things pertaining to life and godliness, that You have even given me Your precious Holy Spirit to guide and empower my life, I am ashamed of my carnal attitude. Forgive me, Lord. Let the song of praise and thanksgiving toward You forever be in my mouth. Amen.

Declare War on Grumbling

God destroyed Israel for its grumbling, murmuring and complaining against Moses. A church split or division almost always has a grumbling element as one of its roots.

In chapter 6 we learned that when Jesus referred to Judas Iscariot as a "devil," He was referring to the generic, impersonal definition of the word *diabolos,* which meant "slanderer" or "malicious gossip." Judas evidently could not keep his negative perspective to himself.

It is not hard to imagine that before Judas betrayed Christ he expressed many criticisms of Jesus to the Pharisees—the final offense being that Jesus allowed an expensive ointment to be "wasted" by it being poured upon His head (see Matthew 26:7). "Why was this perfume not sold for three hundred denarii and given to poor people?" Judas asked indignantly (John 12:5). His attitude actually led a minor insurrection against Jesus, causing indignation to spread among the other apostles as well (see Matthew 26:8). Who permitted this thoughtless luxury? Jesus did. Who reaped its immediate benefits? Again, the answer is Jesus. Perhaps in Judas' critical mind the last straw before betraying Jesus was that He did not apologize for this apparent "misuse of funds" but instead defended the extravagant act.

Betrayal is never a sudden thing; rather, it is an accumulative response to unresolved anger, disappointment or jealousy one feels toward another. The offenses we do not transfer to God in surrendered prayer inevitably decay and become a poison within our spirits. This poison is then transferred to others through slander. We feel justified, yet actually we have become malicious gossips. We feel we are serving the cause of "truth," when in fact we have become enemies to the cause of love.

A Problem with Grumbling

To understand the betrayal of Christ we must descend into its source: a grumbling spirit. When we lose sight of the many things for which we should be thankful, we become murmurers and grumblers, increasingly absorbed with a thought-life born in hell. Remember: Lucifer found fault with God in heaven! Paradise is not even enough for a grumbling spirit!

Beware when your anger toward another Christian leads you to gossip about him, especially if he is a church leader. If you do, then you are no longer being conformed to Christ but to the one who delivered Him up.

Of course, this grumbling attitude was not isolated to Judas. Many would-be disciples and Jewish leaders also were infected with it. Even after witnessing Jesus' many miracles, including the supernatural feeding of the five thousand, a large crowd began to find fault.

"Do not grumble among yourselves," Jesus warned (John 6:43). Yet they persisted. These were not just people who

did not know Christ. These were His very disciples, and
they were not grumbling at a sinner but at the only sin-
less man who ever lived. "But Jesus, conscious that His
disciples grumbled at this, said to them, 'Does this cause
you to stumble?'" (John 6:61). Yet still the grumbling spirit
continued, until "many of His disciples withdrew and were
not walking with Him anymore" (John 6:66).

Grumbling caused people to stop seeing miracles, become offended by Christ's words and stop walking with
Him. As it was then, so it is today. Grumbling will ultimately cause a person to stop walking with Jesus. It is a
killer. Incredibly, the early disciples (not just the Pharisees)
found fault with the Son of God! They had heaven in their
midst and could not see it. That is what a grumbling attitude can do.

This poison is prevalent in the Church today. I tell you
plainly: God does not want a grumbling people to represent
Him on earth. If we are habitually gossiping, grumbling or
complaining, we should beware: The path we are on leads
away from Christ.

The Thankful Heart

Personally, I have declared war on grumbling. I have
declared that an unthankful heart is an enemy of God's
will. Can you join me in this? Can you crucify a murmuring spirit? We have received too much from God to allow
ourselves opportunities for unbelief. We have received too
many gifts and privileges to allow a grumbling, murmuring
heart to disqualify us from our destinies.

In contrast, the thankful heart sees the best part of every
situation. It sees problems and weaknesses as opportunities,
struggles as refining tools, and sinners as saints in progress.
My prayer, dear ones, is for each of us to possess the abundant life that Jesus came to give us. I want to wrestle that

little, ugly, grumbling thing off your soul and put a living awareness of the goodness of God in its place!

The very quality of our lives decays as we murmur. Paul warned, "Nor let us . . . grumble, as [Israel] did, and were destroyed by the destroyer" (1 Corinthians 10:9, 10). Every time we open ourselves to grumbling, our lives open up to destruction.

Paul wrote, "Whatever is true, whatever is honorable, . . . right, . . . pure, . . . lovely, . . . if there is any excellence and if anything worthy of praise, dwell on these things" (Philippians 4:8). If your mind is fixed on something other than the wonderful life of God, then it is not "fixed"; it is broken. God wants to give us a new attitude. You say, "Who is going to take care of finding all the things that are wrong?" Oh, there are plenty of volunteers for that. Better to ask, "How can I attain the blessed life Jesus came to give me?"

A Blessed Family and Future

Some of us cannot communicate with our loved ones. Why? Part of the reason is that we are unappreciative of them. You see, just as God requires us to "enter His gates with thanksgiving" (Psalm 100:4), so we gain access and the "right to speak" into the hearts of our loved ones through genuinely appreciating the good things we see within them. We must learn to be thankful for the people God has given us.

If you are not thankful for your teenagers, for example, your disappointment with them will ultimately drive them from you. Take time with them and sincerely communicate the things you appreciate about them. There are many good things about them that they need to hear you acknowledge. I am not saying we should not correct our children, but we must balance correction with appreciation and praise, reinforcing their sense of self-worth and value.

Because God has created us to be social creatures, we are born with an inner desire for acceptance. In fact, we desire acceptance more than righteousness. By appreciating our loved ones, we affirm and settle the search for acceptance that compels them toward ungodly associations. Just as when property "appreciates," increasing in value, so appreciating our loved ones removes destructive tendencies created by self-hatred and fear of rejection. We inspire them to become better, not by continually harping on what is wrong with them, but by clearly appreciating and establishing what is right.

There is something like radar inside the human heart that senses the displeasure of others. Displeasure and ingratitude are like a repellant to human relationships. People think, "If I cannot measure up, if you cannot see anything good in me, I'll go where people will accept me as I am." Thanksgiving, on the other hand, brings our loved ones closer to us, rather than driving them away.

Speaking of the people the Father put in His life, Jesus prayed, "Thine they were, and thou gavest them me" (John 17:6, KJV). One translation reads, "They are your gift to me" (verse 24, NAB). Jesus did not think of His disciples as always falling short or as a hindrance; rather, He welcomed them into His life as a gift of His Father's love. Did they fail Him? Yes. But He was thankful and treated them with reverence and gratitude.

Your loved ones, pastor and church are gifts from God. Tell them you appreciate them. Personally, I am deeply thankful to God for my wife and her love and support. Likewise, I thank God for my children and the people I serve at my church; our pastors, elders and deacons are wonderful people. Are any of them perfect? No, but I appreciate them as gifts from the hand of God Himself.

I know married couples, however, who wind up discussing all that is wrong with their relationship every time they talk intimately. Why not stop talking about it and just do what is right? Do you understand? Ingratitude is "relationship repellant." Thanksgiving, on the other hand, is the doorway to oneness.

We ought to be the happiest, most joyful, earthshaking individuals the world has ever seen. God is for us. He has written our names in the Book of Life! That alone is more than enough to make us invincibly thankful, happy, glad and joyful.

Some of you have been gossiping and grumbling. It is time for a fast. From what? From grumbling. For the next thirty days, each time you are tempted to complain, find something for which to be thankful. Make lists of people and things for which you are thankful to God. Let's put an end to grumbling and complaining and become a people who possess the wonderful life of God!

Lord, deliver me from words that carry gossip. Master, I realize that I, too, at times have betrayed You when I gossiped and grumbled about other Christians. Jesus, create in me a passion to walk in thanksgiving and praise to You. Free me to be an encourager to others. Amen.

Pastoral Safeguards against Division

Pastors, too often we are the cause of the problems in our churches. We are too insecure. We cannot expect a congregation to trust us if we do not trust the Lord. It is time for us to grow up and by God's grace make room for our churches to grow as well.

To the senior pastor or leader: How do we remedy the relational tragedy of divisions and church splits? Certainly the complexities involved in solving this sin require more information than can be found in a single book, as there are numerous issues and angles to consider. What I have compiled here are some fundamental standards that will help preserve your church from unnecessary divisions.

1. Make it easier for people to transfer to another church. It is admittedly difficult for us pastors to let people go.

But when we do not provide creative, gracious ways for people to move on, they are left with no alternative and feel forced to rebel against us. In war, even enemies exchange prisoners; how much more should the Body of Christ implement loving ways to release individuals? Remember: God thought it fitting that there would be four gospels—four different ways of expressing the good news of Jesus Christ. Likewise, people need variety. So do not let your insecurities make it hard for people to move on.

2. Provide a clear understanding of the spiritual authority structure in your church. Some of us feel awkward teaching about our authority as pastors. Yet we will have problems if we are vague about our church government. You do not have to be "authoritarian" to teach on authority. God gives us authority to protect, guide, correct and console those whom we love. We have authority to liberate but not dominate. Let the church members understand why Christ gives leaders authority and why it is important to their growth to submit to those leaders and obey them (see Hebrews 13:17). The flow of authority should be plainly stated in a brochure or handout that people receive when they join the church. And during times of turbulence, clarity concerning the governmental structure can help people avoid siding with those engendering division.

3. Before accepting a call to a local church, make sure you understand where final authority resides in that church. In some churches, directional leadership does not rest with the pastor but with the elder or deacon board. On occasion, this board is not seeking a senior leader as much as someone who is a good teacher, counselor or administrator. Then when a division arises concerning a change in church direction, the pastor splits the church. This is wrong. No minister

should accept the call to serve a local congregation without also accepting the unique flow of authority in that church. The authority structure should be spelled out clearly in the beginning so there is no misunderstanding.

4. Be honest about your intended use of spiritual gifts. I have known pastors who actually lied when asked by the call committee if they spoke in tongues. Then after a few months of guiding the church, they introduced spiritual gifts against the will of the deacon board. This is a church split waiting to happen.

5. Be accountable to a board or leadership team. Just as you expect your church to submit to your vision and guidance, so should you render yourself genuinely accountable to those who can advise, strengthen and balance your spiritual walk. Any pastor who does not have a board of elders or deacons, or a district supervisor to whom he submits, is asking for division. At the least, a pastor should willingly be accountable concerning his or her moral behavior and doctrine. Additionally, that same leadership team should watch for fatigue or stress in the pastor or pastor's family.

6. Be willing to listen to the advice or suggestions of church members. Some of the best advice I have received came from homemakers in the church. Sometimes what seems like a complaint from a member actually may be the voice of the Lord trying to reveal an area of need we have not addressed. Model humility and openness. It will cut down on members feeling the need to form a posse just to communicate with you.

7. Deal with your insecurities. Paul tells us that God has given a variety of ministries to equip the saints. None of us can meet every human need. Consider how a doctor sends a patient to a specialist—one who is better qualified to remedy a unique physical condi-

tion than he is. He is not so insecure that he cannot enlist another doctor to better serve the patient. He recognizes his limits and gets help. Likewise, we need to admit that we cannot cure or fix every spiritual condition of the people in our churches. If another local pastor has an effective ministry in a certain area, do not be reluctant to send a member to that pastor.

8. Unite with other pastors in the city for prayer, fellowship and healing. God is restoring unity to the citywide church. We can hardly expect our local flock to be united if we ourselves are divided from the larger Body of Christ. We need friends and confidants, people with whom we can be vulnerable and transparent with our needs. Often ministers will suffer the loss of close church friends who for one reason or another actually turn against them. To survive, pastors will pray, "If I have to walk alone, Lord, I will follow You." Such a prayer is helpful during the time of heartache, but it can become like an inner vow that creates a wall of isolation around the minister's heart. We learn to walk alone, as it is less painful; however, it is also less fruitful. It is thus imperative that leaders unite with other pastors, where trust and healing can emerge and pastors themselves can be healed.

9. Be prepared for people in the church to desire ministry opportunities. If our teaching is truly anointed by God, people will grow. How much they grow depends upon the size of their opportunity. Goldfish in a little bowl will grow two or so inches; in a pond they might grow as large as ten or twelve inches. It is the size of the opportunity that often determines the level of growth. As leaders, we should be aware that maturing Christians need opportunities to develop spiritually. How have we provided sanctioned ministry opportunities for upcoming leaders? Are we connected to ministry schools where individu-

als can receive further training? These positive approaches will help people grow without splitting the church.

10. Walk with integrity. I mentioned the following truth in chapter 7, but it is worthy of repeating. When the Babylonians took God's people captive, Jeremiah lamented the destruction of Jerusalem with an insightful yet frightening statement: "The adversary and the enemy could enter the gates of Jerusalem. Because of the sins of her prophets and the iniquities of her priests" (Lamentations 4:12–13). And remember that David's sin of calling for a census caused a plague to fall on Israel. Not until he offered sacrifice in repentance did the plague abate (see 1 Chronicles 21). Habitual, serious sin in your life leaves the church you serve vulnerable to spiritual assault. True spiritual authority is a shelter, comfort and strength to God's people. While no one is perfect, if we walk with serious compromise, the enemy will gain access to our churches through "the sins of her prophets and the iniquities of her priests." What we are fighting outwardly may be what we ourselves caused inwardly by the strongholds of sin in our lives.

11. Stay close to God. Remember: All ministry is first unto the Lord. If you have experienced a church split, your heart probably has been wounded and is in need of healing. Every person God uses has suffered difficulties, rejection, slander and betrayal. Though our hearts are struck and wounded, the Lord desires to restore us and in all these things make us more than conquerors. Just as the Lord restored David's soul, He will restore yours as well as you draw near to Him (see Psalm 23). Take time with Christ daily. After all, this is really about your relationship with Him.

Lord, You said the good shepherd lays down his life for the sheep. Master, I desire to be a good shepherd, one who feeds and cares for Your flock. Lord, heal my heart where I have been wounded or cautious. Let my soul be free to love You fully and serve those You have committed to my care. In Jesus' name. Amen.

A God of Order

For this reason I left you in Crete, that you would set in order what remains.

Titus 1:5

I want to talk about a prominent aspect of the Father's nature and our corresponding need to understand the realm of authority. For some the mere mention of the word *authority* awakens fear, so before we begin let me ask you for grace. Please consider what I present without forming your opinion until I am finished.

The Value of Freedom

First I want to counterbalance my words on authority with another truth concerning our spiritual freedom in Christ. When the Spirit of God begins His transforming work, He starts with individuals. We are not faceless numbers to the Father but beloved children. Indeed, Jesus assures us that His sheep know His voice as He calls them each by name. As unique souls we are important to the Lord. He values us. He hears our individual cries when we pray. He knows our distinct needs when we struggle. And He created us as individuals for a purpose: to walk in true spiritual freedom so that each of us, in full possession of his or her will, can freely choose conformity to the Son of God. Christlikeness is our choice, our liberty and our destiny.

Mankind was created in God's image, and at the core of the divine nature is true, spiritual freedom. As Paul wrote, "It was for freedom that Christ set us free" (Galatians 5:1). We will misunderstand what this chapter is about unless we read it as spiritually free individuals. God does not want us to "look" outwardly righteous yet inwardly be in bondage. He wants us free, in bondage to no one or any thing but God Himself. You see, if our righteousness is only because the pastor or other Christians are looking, we are shallow indeed. Jesus came to set captives free and bring liberty to prisoners (see Isaiah 61:1–2; Luke 4:18–19). God wants each of us to be an individual who in the power of the Holy Spirit has control over his or her mind, will and emotions. He especially does not want us subservient to the intimidations or manipulations of man.

When we discuss order, authority and submission issues, therefore, I pray that you hear my words as free people who have a clear vision of becoming Christlike. As such, you have the right to go to any church or no church at all; you are free to throw this book against a wall or read only what you want. No one can exclude you from a church because from the moment you were born again God enrolled you in the "church of the firstborn," which is in heaven (see Hebrews 12:22–23).

But it is one thing to be assured of salvation; it is another to attain the likeness of Christ. If we will in truth become

Christlike, we must see with revelation the reasons why our Father calls us to honor the order in our local church and why the way to exercising Christlike authority is bowing in Christlike submission.

God Is a God of Order

Having secured ourselves in the freedom given to us in Christ, let us turn our eyes upon the Father. One cannot truly know God or appreciate Him as He is without being awed at the ordered array of His universe. The life we enjoy in its splendor and variety is built upon a substructure of immutable order. The God who created animals, vegetation and people also created the subatomic worlds and the unchanging laws of physics.

When something is "ordered," it is because someone is in authority. We may imagine ourselves in the afterlife enjoying the great pleasures of heaven, but there is authority in heaven also. Heaven itself is ordered with an angelic hierarchy that includes archangels, seraphim, cherubim, thrones, dominions, principalities, powers, virtues and angels. Each of these spirit-beings represents a level of authority in God's Kingdom. Remember: Heaven is not like earth. Most of earth's population follow their own will as they decide life's choices, but in heaven only one will is followed: God's. If you do not like this idea, you cannot go to heaven, for only those who do God's will are going to enter the Kingdom of God (see Matthew 7:21).

Of course, doing God's will unites the reason we were created with the joy of serving the Creator. God matches our gifts and skills with opportunities to fulfill them; and as we accomplish the tasks we were created to fulfill we cannot help but worship Him. But still, only one will is followed.

I am saying this because this same God of order, who created the ordered universe and the hierarchy of angels in heaven, also conceived and designed the Church. In fact, originally "church" was an extension of God's ordered domain: the Kingdom of heaven on earth. Thus, when we read the book of Acts we see that the people in the early Church were part of this ordered domain: united "with one mind" and "with one accord"(Acts 1:14; 4:24; 5:12). Because heaven is ordered and the Lord is a God of order, the Church was an ordered society where authority and submission were simply accepted on earth as it is in heaven.

Unity before Power

One may argue, "If we had their power, we would be united as well." Let me emphasize: They were of one mind *before* Pentecost (see Acts 1:14). If there had not been unity among the disciples prior to Pentecost, there would not have been an outpouring of the Holy Spirit on Pentecost. The outpouring did not create unity; unity made the way for the outpouring. The order was first, then came the power of the Spirit.

This principle of having order before power also can be seen by studying the Israelites, who conquered Canaan, and David, who with his mighty men united Israel and extended her boundaries. In both cases unity preceded power. Central to the empowering of people to attain their destiny was their ability to submit to the leaders God had appointed. Unity simply cannot be sustained without authority and submission.

God Honors Order and Authority

Let me take this a little further. The Lord sits in the heavens and does whatever He pleases, yet repeatedly the Scriptures confirm that He honors the order He has created and works within its protocols. The Lord appeared to Paul, for example, spoke to him, actually blinded him in His glory and then said, "Get up and enter the city, and it will be told you what you must do" (Acts 9:6). Why did the Lord not just tell Paul what to do? Paul had to learn about God, at least initially, as he submitted to other Christian leaders—in this case Ananias, a man who was a Christian before Paul. This is God's order, and the Lord Himself honored it.

Or consider the Roman centurion Cornelius, who would be the first European convert. An angel appeared to him in a dream and told him a man named Simon Peter would explain to him the way of salvation. Why did the angel not simply tell Cornelius about Jesus? Because God had begun the Church with the Jews. Before the Gentiles could enter the Kingdom en masse they would hear of Christ from the Jews, who first accepted the Messiah. God honored the order He created, which was to present the Gospel "to the Jew first and also to the Greek" (Romans 1:16; 2:10).

Church protocol in the book of Acts further exemplifies this honoring of order. When Philip brought the Gospel to Samaria, miracles, conversions and great signs accompanied it. But Philip would not lay his hands upon the Samaritans to receive the Holy Spirit. Why? Because until this time the Holy Spirit had spread only through the hands of the first apostles. God required His servant to respect the order and authority of the first apostles.

Consider the order in Jesus' family. The angel Gabriel spoke to Mary, revealing that through the Holy Spirit she would conceive the Son of God. Yet from the time Mary married Joseph, God spoke only to him concerning direction for the family. Angels assured him that Mary's pregnancy was from God, and later he received dreams and angelic warnings telling him to leave Israel and then when to return. God honored the order of the family—because

Adam was created first, then Eve. Yes, the Lord still works when conditions are out of order because He honors faith. But just because He accommodates our weaknesses, we should not assume He will endorse them with the fullness of His power.

The Example of Christ's Submission

Consider the life of Christ Himself. As a child He grew up "in subjection" to His parents (see Luke 2:51). He also was submissive to the instructions of the rabbis, and as was His custom He faithfully participated in the Sabbath readings at the synagogue (see Luke 4:16). Jesus simply was not a rebel. At the Jordan River He eagerly submitted Himself to the ministry of John the Baptist in order "to fulfill all righteousness," though He was John's spiritual superior. Indeed, it was while He humbled Himself to a lesser ministry that the flood of the Father's pleasure, together with the Holy Spirit, descended upon Him (see Matthew 3:13–17).

I know what I am about to say will seem over the line to many, but Jesus did not instruct His followers to rebel even against false religious authority. Listen to what He taught: "The scribes and the Pharisees have seated themselves in the chair of Moses." On their own, the Pharisees assumed an authority that God had not given them. Yet listen to how Jesus tells His disciples to relate to false authority: "Therefore all that they tell you, do and observe, but do not do according to their deeds; for they say things and do not do them" (Matthew 23:2–3).

Amazingly Jesus instructed both His disciples and the larger multitude to "do and observe" all that the Pharisees taught. I do not believe in any way He intended for His disciples to remain with the Pharisees, but the implication in Jesus' statement is this: As long as you are Jewish and attend Temple services, the Pharisees are in charge. Submit to them, but do not become like them.

Even though their authority was questionable and their behavior hypocritical, He did not say to disrespect them, but rather not to do as they did. Yes, Jesus Himself confronted the Pharisees harshly. But Jesus was not raising up a people to be known for their confrontational attitudes; they were to be known for their strength of character and their love. When Jesus stood before Pilate He showed Himself meek, like a lamb. Pilate challenged Him, "'Do You not know that I have authority to release You, and I have authority to crucify You?' Jesus answered, 'You would have no authority over Me, unless it had been given you from above'" (John 19:10–11).

Jesus knew that all authority in the universe—the very realm of authority—was under the domain of the Father's watchful gaze (see Romans 13:1). While authority itself could be misused, the Father's authority transcended human authority and could with great power override the imperfections of man. Thus, Jesus was not afraid to submit to people who were spiritually less than Himself because He knew God's greater authority would transform injustice to justice.

In the Godhead, the Father exists as God in authority and the Son exists as God in submission. Jesus, you recall, did only the things He saw the Father do. Everything about Christ was an act of obedience and submission. Christ reveals how God submits to God. In this submission is peace; Jesus rested in the Father's watchful gaze. The issues were never between Jesus and other men, but between Himself and the Father.

When Jesus suffered the injustice of His trial, He did not blame Pilate, the Pharisees, His disciples or the multitudes. He did not even blame the devil. Instead Peter tells us that while Jesus was "being reviled, He did not revile in return; while suffering, He uttered no threats, but kept entrusting Himself to Him who judges righteously" (1 Peter 2:23).

Peter uses Christ's example of submission to tell the Church, "Keep your behavior excellent among the Gentiles. . . . Submit yourselves for the Lord's sake to every human institution, whether to a king as the one in authority, or to governors as sent by him for the punishment of evildoers and the praise of those who do right" (1 Peter 2:12–14).

He continues, "Act as free men, and do not use your freedom as a covering for evil, but use it as bondslaves of God. Honor all people, love the brotherhood, fear God, honor the king. Servants, be submissive to your masters with all respect, not only to those who are good and gentle, but also to those who are unreasonable" (1 Peter 2:16–18).

Did Christ's faith work? Of course! In the first century the cross was the symbol of torture, death and utter hopelessness. But because Jesus trusted the Father's authority to override the misuse of authority, the cross today is the symbol of redemption, resurrection and hope.

Beloved, the Lord is a God of order, and for His purposes He requires that we submit to authority and order—whether it is in the secular world, the family or the church. Listen carefully: Rebellion is not a virtue. Submission was clearly the pattern in Jesus' life. He revealed how God would submit to God, and in so doing He set the pattern for us, who are created in His image.

Lord, forgive me for my insolence toward those in authority. I confess that I have not trusted or understood the realm of authority, but I ask that You forgive me. Help me to ever keep my eyes upon You, trusting Your ability to take my submitted, believing heart through every injustice and into the realm of redemption and power. In Jesus' name. Amen.

Christlike Submission

Our submission to authority is not born of fear or intimidation. True submission comes from revelation and an understanding of the character of Jesus Christ. Submission to godly authority can actually be a means of accelerated growth and imparted grace.

Jesus had full possession of His soul. He did not react to man; He fully trusted God. He could submit to man's frail systems and miscarriages of authority, knowing the Father ultimately would judge righteously and transform the injustice. Where Lucifer demanded full independence from the authority of God, Jesus perfectly yielded to the Father's authority (see 2 Corinthians 13:4).

Facing Our Fears Regarding Submission

Now I know that some are afraid to embrace a submissive attitude toward other men, especially when those men are miscarrying authority. They worry that they will have to submit blindly to the Antichrist or be forced, cult-like, into all manner of sin. We have only to consider the recent sex scandals in the Catholic Church and the misuse of authority among the priests to shudder with legitimate concern.

So let me reinforce this truth: Jesus never submitted to authority that would cause Him to sin, nor did He expect His disciples to sin if one in authority ordered them. Just as you *choose* to submit, so you *choose* not to submit to one telling you to sin. If your employer asks you to lie for him, you can maintain a submissive attitude while telling him, "No, I cannot do that." Yet even in such an instance the motive is not to rebel against man but to submit on a higher level to God.

Another fear is that by submitting to another person we will lose ourselves and become like him or her. But in fact, when we submit to the anointing upon a person we gain more than we invest. Elisha received a double portion of Elijah's anointing because he passionately and faithfully submitted himself to his mentor's anointing. Bear in mind, Elijah was the opposite personality type of Elisha. Yet by submitting he doubled the accomplishments of Elijah.

You see, what we possess of spiritual power is already ours, but it is limited. By putting ourselves in submission to another, we gain some measure of the other person's anointing. Elisha did not lose his own identity by submitting; he did not become a "little Elijah." He still retained his own personality and approach to ministry—except when his ministry began he had twice as much power.

We fear that by being submissive we will be asked to give more than we receive. Again the opposite is true. Jesus taught, "He who receives a prophet in the name of a prophet shall receive a prophet's reward" (Matthew 10:41). Submission is the vehicle for receiving. God rewards a prophet not only in the world to come but also here on earth. The "prophet's reward" represents the unique power dimension a man or woman of God has purchased with sacrifice and suffering. Just by submitting ourselves, by humbly "receiving" from them, we can obtain without cost a measure of the prophet's reward.

Remember: The multitudes did not know Jesus was the Son of God. They did not understand that "by His stripes" they would be healed (Isaiah 53:5, NKJV). They did just one thing: They submitted to Christ for healing and received the "prophet's reward." The Pharisees, on the other hand, did not receive Christ; thus, their unsubmitted attitude disqualified them from receiving the benefits of Jesus' power.

The Wise Person Submits

When a church submits to me, I assume an added responsibility. It does not mean that I as a leader control their now mindless lives. How opposite the truth is! People submitted to my authority are those for whom I pray more frequently. When they are sick I visit them. When they weep I cry with them. And where they are immature I give myself to training them, instructing them in the mysteries of life. The submitted person is the beneficiary of the relationship, much more than the one in authority.

We have seen the abuses of authority, and it has made many of us wary and resistant to the true benefits of submission and impartation. But let's take this a step further. You do not actually need to have a man or woman of God in front of you to be submitted to their anointing. When I was a young man and new in Christ, I would take books by Andrew Murray or Watchman Nee, then kneel at the foot of my bed and read their words. I often felt that I was drinking in, through the Holy Spirit, the substance of their anointing. I did not just read their words; I submitted myself to their teaching.

So consider submission to be the free choice of a wise person who sees something Christlike in another's life and asks to receive it. Submission does not diminish us; it doubles us. It extends the boundaries of our spirituality into the lives of people whom we see have been transformed by Christ—and allows what they have received from Him to be imparted to us as well.

Lord, what a storehouse of riches Your Church is! To think that when You ascended on high, You gave gifts to men, spiritual leaders, who could advance my spiritual growth simply by my submission. Master, let my eyes be ever on You and let me follow men only as they follow You. In Jesus' name. Amen.

The Power of Biblical Honor

> Practice showing honor for just one month to those in authority over you and to those in submission to you. Honor will transform your world.

In a world where "every intent of the thoughts of [mankind's] heart was only evil continually" (Genesis 6:5), Noah walked "blameless in his time" (Genesis 6:9). Noah was a righteous man whose integrity and depth of character contradicted his culture.

Noah faithfully resisted temptation and the pressure to sin. He preached righteousness and spoke boldly against evil. Aware that the end of his world was near, he continued preaching repentance for 120 years. Throughout his life he never wavered; although his words converted no one, he never quit. Among all who lived in his generation, Noah alone found favor with God.

Then Noah's eyes beheld the terrible descent of the wrath of God; his ears heard the terrifying, final cries of an entire civilization. His mind experienced the horrifying destruction of every man, woman and child outside the ark. What burden does such an experience create upon the human soul? What nightmares?

We do not know how Noah processed the catastrophic end of his world, but we do know that after the flood a second genesis began with Noah. He farmed and planted a vineyard. From the harvest he produced juice, which fermented into wine. It is not clear if this was the first time he, or any man, tasted the effects of wine. But he drank it, and it made him so drunk that he collapsed in his tent, unconscious and naked in a drunken stupor (see Genesis 9:20–21).

Here was a righteous preacher who for whatever reason had fallen short of his own high standards. Into this scene comes Ham, one of his three sons. Ham entered Noah's tent and saw the shameful state of his father. Instead of silently covering his father, Ham reported the scene to his two brothers. Ham's motive was not to discreetly cover his father's shame, but rather to expose it (see verse 22).

His brothers, Shem and Japheth, were of a different spirit. They took a garment and, walking backward with it on their shoulders, covered their father. Keep this point in mind: Ham dishonored his father by seeking to expose his shame; Shem and Japheth honored their father by covering his weakness. When Noah discovered what had occurred, he cursed Ham's descendants because of what Ham had done, and he proclaimed blessings and prosperity upon Shem and Japheth (see verses 23–27).

The lesson for us is profound: Our future and the future of our children is attached to how well we understand the value of honor and the curse that follows us when we exploit the imperfections of those in authority over us.

American Culture

I want to talk to you about honor and dishonor in America. But first let me state that I love America, I fast for this nation, and I carry an unceasing burden of prayer for her and her leaders. When some Christians have in the past anticipated America's destruction, I have wept for America's revival. I believe Americans are a generous, often self-sacrificing, freedom-loving people. Additionally, this nation has stood with Israel and has extended its hands to the poor of the world. I also believe many of our forefathers were Christians who, as they knelt upon the sands of the New World, dedicated this land and its future to God.

Yet frankly, America's love for freedom has led us across moral boundaries. Today we demand—and our courts protect—all manner of immorality under free speech provisions. The unborn are denied the freedom of life itself for the sake of a woman's "freedom of choice." Our insatiable lusts have created a caricature of freedom that is unbalanced by responsibility and untempered by heaven's authority. For many, we are not "One Nation Under God," but "One Nation Under Freedom." Increasingly in America, freedom has become its own god.

Some of this can be traced to the justifiable reaction of our founding fathers as they rebelled against the tyranny of European kings and bishops. Reaching to create a land free of authoritarianism certainly was noble. In our rejection of the cultural traditions of the past, however, we have minimized the power of honor that existed in older cultures.

Nations are not only governed by laws but also unique societal mores. In Asian nations, honor and respect preside over societies; people bow when greeting one another as a sign of honor. For Germanic nations, discipline and obedience set boundaries. For Americans, liberty is the identifying trait. Yet when the core standard of a people is freedom itself, whatever virtues restrain freedoms (such as self-denial, honor or compliance) often are devalued as flaws.

As a result, a society that learns to minimize honor minimizes the positive effect the principles of honor have upon its basic institutions. It is precisely because of the lack of honor that our institutions of family, church and school have suffered unprecedented breakdowns over the past half century.

"Don't Tread on Me"

The early pioneers came to America looking for the New World. Their DNA remains a constant motive in the American psyche: Americans are still looking for a new world. We tend to live at the frontier of change—new ideas, new philosophies and new trends. Today in many ways we have become one huge reaction to authority and tradition. We are not happy unless we are pushing the boundaries and breaking the limits. "No rules" has become the rallying cry for a spirit that infects our culture.

In truth the seeds of this defiant attitude were sown long ago, even before this nation officially broke from England. Consider the Gadsden Flag. During the Revolutionary War, perhaps more than many other flags, this banner embodied the sentiment of a host of patriots. In fact, Benjamin Franklin pushed to have this flag represent the spirit of the new republic. What was the Gadsden Flag? It was a coiled serpent with the inscription "Don't tread on me."

You will recall that Jesus specifically told His disciples they would "tread on serpents" (Luke 10:19). Christ's statement is a reference to the Garden of Eden, where the Lord promised that the seed of the woman, Christ, would tread upon the head of the serpent. Yet woven into the fabric of the American culture is this brazen defiance: "Don't tread on me." Was this banner merely the symbol of rebellion against England, or did it embody a rebellion against anyone, including Christ Himself?

Even among the early American Christians there existed a strong independent heart attitude. Most of our first ancestors came from "Protestant" stock—"those who protest." Not only had they protested the perceived errors of Catholicism, but during various eras Protestants persecuted and protested each other as well. Their legacy of visible, vocal dissent as a means of change has been structured into America's subconscious so that even today, to protest is to walk a heroic path. It is to follow those who for the sake of their principles—and often at the cost of their lives—defied the authority of a king or bishop.

Thus, confrontation emerged in America as a means through which change materialized. Let us not fail to defend the virtue that fearlessly speaks against true evil. Yet too often we find ourselves protesting when, instead, we could have humbly and civilly discussed issues that needed change.

I am saying that "confrontational spirituality" has been carried to excess in the Church and often is the spark that ignites the fire of division and splits. I am not denying that there are times we need to confront a situation or person. But there are far too many of us who, thinking we are the spiritual sons of the Old Testament prophets, are simply critical and confrontational by nature.

God Calls Us to Honor Others

This is especially troublesome when we consider New Testament Scriptures that in fact call us to the exact opposite approach in our relationships. God calls us to honor and respect people, even when we disagree with them. Peter admonishes:

Honor all people, love the brotherhood, fear God, honor the king. Servants, be submissive to your masters with all respect.

1 Peter 2:17–18

Honor all people? Honor the king? Servants, be submissive with respect? Surely this apostolic leader is not speaking to the Church in America! We want our rights! We are not afraid of any man, be he king or priest. Yes, but the issue is not whether we are afraid; it is whether or not we are capable of showing genuine honor in obedience to God's Word.

There is something within us that grates at the idea of honoring people. We say—often quite righteously—we will honor only God. We feel it is our task to keep others humble, lest their pride take over. In reality it is our pride that has taken over, not theirs; it is fueled by our jealousy of another's success.

God calls us to honor all men for the simple fact that He chose to give them life. Jesus lived and died so sinful men could be saved. People are precious to the Father. Yes, the person standing before you today may be a sinner, but by showing honor you tell that person that he or she is important to the Almighty.

Some people we honor for their attainments; others we honor for their intrinsic worth to God. Yet the call of God is to honor all. We do not honor the actions of sinners but the humanity of sinners. We are not to worship people, as those who swoon over celebrities; but we are to show all men honor.

You cannot lead someone to Christ whom you have dishonored. You cannot sincerely communicate the love of God if you do not respect the person to whom you are speaking. Our tradition of dishonoring people has not come from God. In fact, the Kingdom of God emerges with a completely opposite spirit. The Kingdom is a culture graced

with honor and respect for the dignity of all people, which
Jesus demonstrated repeatedly by the honor He showed
the often-maligned Samaritans.

Within the Body of Christ we are commanded to honor
every member, actually giving to the unseemly members more abundant honor (see 1 Corinthians 12:23–24).
We also are called to "honor all people" and "honor the
king" (1 Peter 2:17). We are additionally required to honor
the church elders (see 1 Timothy 5:17); and at work we
should honor and respect those who are our employers (see
1 Timothy 6:1). We are to honor widows (see 1 Timothy 5:3),
spouses (see 1 Peter 3:7, Ephesians 5:33, AMP), the unseemly
(see 1 Corinthians 12:23–25) and the aged (see Leviticus
19:32). In fact, when the elderly enter a room we are told to
stop talking, stand and acknowledge with reverence their
entrance (see Leviticus 19:32). How rare this is in America
today!

The Lord Himself bestows honor on people. John 12:26
says, "If anyone serves Me, the Father will honor him." And
Psalm 91:14–15 says, "Because he has loved Me . . . I will
rescue him and honor him." So if the Lord has no problem
honoring people, considering His great glory, why are we
so apt to dishonor each other?

The word *honor* in Greek means "to fix valuation, esteem by implication and to revere." We must esteem and
fix value to each other. Picture a home where the children
revere their parents and the husband and wife honor each
other. Honor creates a spiritual buffer against the enemy's
attacks, which otherwise erode the quality of our lives.

Moreover, honor releases the power of God, while dishonor greatly hinders it. Jesus taught, "'A prophet is not
without honor except in his hometown and in his own
household.' And He did not do many miracles there because of their unbelief" (Matthew 13:57–58). The people
of Jesus' hometown did not honor Him, and Jesus called
their lack of honor "unbelief," for which cause He could

do no miracles. In other words, when we dishonor a man or woman of God, we shut down the power of God from working through him or her.

The Ability to Advance in Life

Paul reminds us of the fourth commandment: "Honor your father and mother . . . that it may be well with you" (Ephesians 6:2–3). With that truth in mind, let's return to the story of Noah. When Ham dishonored his father by exposing him, Noah cursed Canaan, the son of Ham. Why didn't Noah curse Ham instead of Ham's son? As Ham had been to Noah, so Canaan would be to Ham. Noah's curse was profound. He said Canaan would be "a servant of servants" (Genesis 9:25). Why? Because if you cannot honor an imperfect leader, you will have continual difficulty advancing in life. You will always be wrestling with poverty.

There are no leaders other than imperfect leaders. Your employer or boss, your pastor or teacher, your mayor, your father or mother—they all are imperfect. When we expose them to humiliation or dishonor by telling others of their weaknesses, it brings a curse upon us. We will never advance in life with such an attitude.

To be successful we need to be able to submit to leaders who are imperfect without dishonoring them. Again I am not saying we are to submit to leaders who have committed serious sexual sin or crimes worthy of imprisonment, but we should not have qualms about submitting to men and women who are simply imperfect.

You may say, "If I do that, I will feel like a hypocrite, a 'yes' man." If you do not show honor, you are already a hypocrite, for a true Christian esteems and respects people. You do not have to trust them, but you must honor and respect them.

This does not mean you should not have concerns when you see a problem. You may indeed have good advice or even a revelation to share that can help your leader. But do not open the door to dishonoring leaders, especially in the Church! If you see a problem, do not follow Ham's example. Do not go telling your brothers; instead, cover the situation in love. Follow the procedure Jesus gives us in Matthew 18, remaining respectful and humble as you seek to bring an end to sin in a person's life.

Perhaps you have difficulty advancing in life. Is it possible that you had a dishonoring spirit toward your parents, teachers or others in authority over you, and in a moment of anger they spoke a curse over you—"You are a loser, you will never amount to anything"? You have been blaming them, but the real cause has been your dishonoring attitude.

Today that curse can be broken. Ask God to forgive you for not relating with honor to imperfect authority. Learn to pray for those over you when you see their imperfections, covering them with the blood of Christ. Become one who covers instead of exposes their weakness.

Remember: The future generations of Ham became slaves. How you relate to the imperfections of those in authority determines not only your future, but also the future of your children and your children's children. Do they hear you complain about your boss? Do they listen when you criticize your pastor? Is a curse being passed on to them when they are forced by proximity to hear you slander those in authority? Do you see this? You are actually teaching them how *not* to succeed in life. A dishonoring spirit will cause them to remain needy, frustrated and outside the realm of the blessed and prosperous.

Your children are patterning their lives after you. When you see a need in a leader, pray for that person. Let your children see you praying, and demonstrate how they can handle the imperfections of life. As they watch your redemptive approach to life's difficult issues, they have a chance to learn how Christ Himself dealt with human failure. Will they become bitter and angry at life's structure of authority? Or will they be free to relate to imperfect authorities over them and do so with honor? Are you breeding generations of slaves or generations of free men and women?

> *Lord Jesus, we see how You honored the poor, the sick and the downtrodden. You also did not turn away Your disciples or shame them when they failed. Instead You empowered Your leaders with Your covering love and asked them to show that same love to others. Lord, grant us the grace to honor all men, and so reveal Your love to our world. Amen.*

Are You Currently in a Church Split?

For I am afraid that perhaps when I come I may find you to be not what I wish and may be found by you to be not what you wish; that perhaps there will be strife, jealousy, angry tempers, disputes, slanders, gossip, arrogance, disturbances.

2 Corinthians 12:20

If you are considering splitting your church, then I suggest you set up special seating in your new sanctuary, for you are about to make permanent residents of the spirits of strife, anger and suspicion. They may not show up immediately, but with limited exceptions these spirits will abide in your assembly until you face what you did wrong in splitting a church. Only after you renounce your sin and seek forgiveness from God and your parent congregation will you be victorious over these demonic influences.

"Wait," you say. "You're being harsh, Francis." No, I am being honest. I am telling you what I have seen over and over again throughout the Body of Christ. If you are the leader of a church that split from another group, listen to me carefully: You cannot justify criticism, gossip and division against your former pastor and then suppose those in your present church will not learn from your example. A leader will rise up who will be just like you. He will follow in your footsteps and use your approach to starting a church to justify his approach—only then you will be the one suffering the split.

Jesus put it like this: "By your standard of measure, it will be measured to you" (Matthew 7:2). Paul warned, "Do not be deceived, God is not mocked; for whatever a man sows, this he will also reap" (Galatians 6:7). You cannot sow the wind without reaping the whirlwind (see Hosea 8:7). God does not have to send meteors to punish us; sin carries its own punishment.

Although a splitting group launches into its future with songs of faith and joy, it is a baby marred by a birth defect. It is a church conceived by ambition and born in strife without the blessing of its parent. It may not happen immediately, but usually within three to five years it will suffer its own split and remain more vulnerable to splits than other churches.

You see, within the spiritual DNA of a split church there exists a hidden code, a programmed life pattern, which will continually reanimate each time an ambitious or critical leader rises in the group. Regardless of what doctrines the split church espouses about unity, the "encoded split pattern" exists in the marrow of the church. It is waiting for the right conditions to burst again into strife.

Let me say it again: *Until the sin of division, of being part of a split, is acknowledged and then renounced, until forgiveness is sought from God and the offended congregation, the split pattern will always remain an option in your present church. You cannot sow the wind without reaping the whirlwind.*

If you are currently involved in a division that is rapidly moving toward a split, then I advise you to stop immediately and seek arbitration from spiritual leaders whom you and the parent church respect. If you have been in a split and are part of the church that left, then I urge you to contact your former church and ask for forgiveness. It may not be feasible to reunite; however, a time of forgiveness and prayer together between the two congregations, and perhaps partaking of Communion—even praying the blessing of the Lord upon each other—will bring much healing and closure to the conflict.

If you were part of the parent church that suffered the split, no one has suffered more during this time than your pastor. Within the first three months after the split, a time of honoring your pastor and his or her family will bring great healing to them and yourselves. It is also vital that you forgive the offending group, lest a root of bitterness spring up and many be defiled (see Hebrews 12:15).

Some leaders feel there should be little or no contact between the two groups until a cooling-off period passes. Emotions have been shredded, hearts are wounded and much misunderstanding exists. There is a time to talk and another time to turn to God and heal. This cooling-off period should be a time to find new grace from God. If you lost people to a splintered group, you will be tempted to focus on the past, wishing the division and split never happened. Yet you cannot go forward while you are looking back. You need to refocus on the call and purpose of God for your church and press on. After you have forgiven the split group, give the entire matter to the Lord. What you give over, He will take over.

Even as you mourn the loss of friends, remember: Jesus Himself is praying, not only for healing, but also for oneness in the Body of Christ. Letting go of the sorrow is as much a step of faith as trusting God to bring reconciliation.

Finally, in all things you must let your love triumph. This is really about God expanding your capacity to show mercy. You must let this bad experience work for you. God is good, and you must believe in order to see "the goodness of the LORD in the land of the living" (Psalm 27:13).

> *Lord, in holy fear I come to You. I acknowledge before You that division is sin. I renounce participating in a carnal division and ask that You forgive me and those whom I may have wounded by my actions. I forgive those in the other group and ask, blessed Lord, that even in this You would perfect my heart. In Jesus' name. Amen.*

Part 4

Becoming Christlike

The one who says he abides in Him
ought himself to walk
in the same manner as He walked.

1 John 2:6

True Success

That I may know Him and the power of His resurrection and the fellowship of His sufferings, being conformed to His death; in order that I may attain to the resurrection from the dead.

Philippians 3:10–11

In a real sense this book is not about ending divisions; it is about the Church becoming Christlike. Unity is the consequence of Christlikeness. If our goal is something other than conformity to Christ, inevitably we will be left vulnerable to deception and divisions. And when I speak of becoming Christlike I mean a few specific, love-motivated realities, such as humility, submissiveness, intercessory prayer and a mature, redemptive attitude of heart.

True Humility

Beloved, all of us need to seek God for a true revelation of Christ's humility. Jesus said the humble are "the greatest" in His Kingdom (Matthew 18:4). In the Church today, among leaders and congregations alike, we need the humility Jesus demonstrated when He girded Himself and washed His disciples' feet (see John 13:4–5). This is not an imposed humility but a choice we make as we seek the nature of the Savior.

Paul tells us to have the same attitude that we see in Christ who, existing in the form of God, did not regard His equality with the Father as a thing to be grasped but emptied Himself of His privileges and in humility took the form of a man—and then died for men (see Philippians 2:5–8)! In other words, Jesus saw the need—as terrible as it was—and came to redeem it. He could have simply destroyed the earth; He could have ignored our need. Instead He died for us. His footsteps are the will of God for me. With all my heart I desire to walk as He did—without fear, motivated by love, empowered to make a difference and willing to die for those who would crucify me.

Submissiveness

When I speak of becoming Christlike, it includes being submissive to authority. Jesus grew up in subjection to His parents; He insisted on submitting Himself to John's baptism, though He was clearly John's spiritual superior. He submitted Himself to the injustice of Pilate's secular authority, while entrusting Himself without fear to the power of the Father who judges righteously. Christ's eyes were not on Pilate but upon the Father who, in His omnipotence, would soon take every injustice and make it part of the plan of redemption. So Jesus could submit to man because He had faith in God the Father.

When we make our goal the meekness and submissiveness of Christ, we know we can trust God with our future. Then we have no problem serving the vision and ministry of someone else along the way. And ambition, a cause of so many church splits, has no power or place among us.

Prayer and a Redemptive Heart Attitude

To seek Christlikeness means that when I see something wrong in the born-again church, I am capable of looking at it maturely without panic. Because I am a person of prayer, I trust that God has a redemptive answer. Do you recall how Jesus handled the demon-possessed man in Gerasenes? The individual confronted Jesus as He passed among the tombs; broken chains dragged from his wrists and ankles. Yet within minutes Jesus had restored the man to his right mind, delivering him of the tormenting evil spirits that possessed him (see Mark 5:1–15). The same Jesus who calmed the demoniac dwells in us. He does not want us to be swallowed up by what is wrong; He calls us to transform it.

My call to you, beloved, is to walk as Christ walked, in humility and submission, so we can present to Him a Church without spot or blemish or any such thing (see Ephesians 5:27). Let us persevere in trials, knowing that God sees and judges. Let us define success not merely as having a name known on earth, but attaining Christlikeness and possessing a name known and honored in heaven.

> *Lord Jesus, I see in You all I want to be. I desire with all my heart to be like You, Lord. You have promised that a pupil shall become like his master. Fulfill Your promise in me! Transform me, so the world will see and worship You. Help me to define true success as attaining one goal: possessing Your glorious nature. Amen.*

Unoffendable

> I will give you a new heart and put a new spirit within you;
> and I will remove the heart of stone from your flesh and
> give you a heart of flesh.
>
> Ezekiel 36:26

God has a new heart for us that cannot be offended—an
"unoffendable" heart. Beloved, possessing an unoffendable
heart is not an option or a luxury; it is not a little thing.

Jesus warns that as we near the end of the age a majority
of people will be offended to such a degree that they fall
away from the faith. Listen carefully to His warning:

> Then shall many be offended, and shall betray one another,
> and shall hate one another. . . . And because iniquity shall
> abound, the love of many shall wax cold.
>
> Matthew 24:10, 12, KJV

"Many" will be offended; the love of "many" will grow cold. My prayer is that we will hear His words with holy fear.

The Danger of Harboring Offense

When we allow an offense to ferment in our hearts, it causes serious spiritual consequences. In the above verse Jesus named three dangerous results: betrayal, hatred and cold love. When we are offended by someone, if we cannot genuinely forgive him or her and put the incident in the hands of the Lord, we should go to the individual. If we do not approach him or her, our unresolved woundedness begins to move our hearts away from intimacy with that person and toward betrayal; we find ourselves talking maliciously behind his or her back. Our conversation is sprinkled with subtle, negative "hints" that expose the of-fending individual's weaknesses to others. We may mask our betrayal by saying we are just looking for advice or counsel, but when we look back we see we have spoken negatively about that person to far too many people. Our real goal was not to get spiritual help for ourselves but to seek revenge toward the one who offended us. How is such action not a manifestation of hatred? An offended soul leads to cold love, which unfolds into betrayal and hatred.

People do not usually stumble over boulders; they stum-ble over stones—relatively small things. It may be that the personality of someone in authority bothers us and soon we are offended. Or a friend or family member fails to meet our expectations and we take an offense into our soul. Beloved, if we will "endure to the end" (Matthew 24:13), we will have to confront the things that bother us.

When Jesus warns that we need endurance, He is saying that it is easier to begin the race than finish it. Between now and the day you die you will face major times of offense that you will need to overcome. You might be in such a time right now. Do not minimize the danger of harboring an offense.

No one plans on falling away; no one ever says, "Today, I think I'll try to develop a hardened, cold heart." Such things enter our souls through stealth, and it is only naiveté that assumes it could not happen to us. I know many people who consistently become offended about one thing or another. Instead of dealing with the offenses, these people carry them until the weight disables their walk with God. You may be doing fine today, but I guarantee you that tomorrow something will happen that will inevitably disappoint or wound you; some injustice will strike you, demanding you retaliate in the flesh.

The Root of Offense

An offense can strike at our virtues or our sins, our values or our pride. It can penetrate and wound any dimension of the soul. I once taught a series of messages about gossip. Most people saw their sin and repented, but a core group of gossips was greatly offended and ultimately left the church. Truthfully, most of the time I have no idea who specifically needs to hear what I am teaching, but God knows. And when the Holy Spirit exposes sin in someone's soul and the person refuses the opportunity to repent, he or she often becomes offended at the person who brought the teaching. Instead of humbling our hearts, we are outraged at the pastor or teachers in the church.

Paul told Timothy to "reprove, rebuke, exhort" (see 2 Timothy 4:2). He did not say, "exhort, exhort, exhort," but exhortation is what we receive in most churches. People do not change by exhortation alone. Certainly we need to be encouraged, but there are also times, beloved, when we need to be reproved and rebuked. There are areas in all of us that need to be confronted and disciplined.

Today there are preachers who are afraid to preach truth for fear people will react and leave the church. The end result is a church of easily offended people who cannot grow beyond their inability to accept correction. The leader who refuses to discipline and correct those in sin is in disobedience to God. He or she is unable to lead people into any truly transforming changes in their lives; they will not "endure to the end" if they cannot be corrected (see Matthew 24:13).

We need to become a people who say, "Lord, show me what needs to change in me." I am talking about growing up. A wise man will receive a rebuke and will prosper. But a fool rejects his father's discipline (see Proverbs 15:5).

Personal Offense

An offense can wound our pride when we are not recognized for our good works or ministry. This happened to my wife and me long ago in California. We were young pastors at a conference when the main leader decided to personally greet each minister and wife. He greeted the couple on our right and then turned to his staff to ask a question. A moment later he returned but passed us by and went to the couple on our left. Everyone around us saw we were bypassed. We were embarrassed and offended. But my wife wisely observed that we could allow this thing to hurt us or we could see it as an investment in sensitivity toward other people's feelings. The offense taught us how others feel when they are ignored. Do you see this? You must make an offense become an opportunity to become more Christlike.

The occasions for taking offense are practically endless. We are daily given the opportunity to either be offended by something or to possess an unoffendable heart. The Lord's promise is that He has given us a new heart: a soft, entreatable heart that can be filled with His Spirit and abound with His love.

> *Lord, forgive me for being so easily offended and for carrying offenses. Father, my heart is foolish and weak. Grant me the unoffendable heart of Jesus Christ. Amen.*

Nothing Causes Them
to Stumble

*Then shall many be offended, and shall betray one another,
and shall hate one another. . . . And because iniquity shall
abound, the love of many shall wax cold.*

Matthew 24:10, 12, KJV

In the last chapter we looked at the lethal effect an offended spirit has upon our lives. We discussed how the only way not to be permanently offended is to attain the unoffend-able heart of Jesus Christ.

Attaining Christ's heart is not a minor issue. Remember: Jesus warned that in the last days "many" would be of-fended. But there is a difference between being wounded and being offended. Frequently we will be wounded by an insensitive remark or injustice that occurs. But a "wounded spirit" is not the same thing as an "offended spirit."

An offended spirit occurs when we do not process our wounds in a Christlike manner. An offended spirit, left unattended and brooding in our minds, will soon manifest as betrayal, hatred and cold love. Jesus said offenses would be the ultimate cause that would lead many to fall from faith. Listen well: Jesus linked the real cause of apostasy not to wrong doctrines, but to wrong reactions.

Are not right doctrines important? Of course, but we can have right information and still have a wrong response. Doctrinal information can be upgraded and refined, but Proverbs warns that someone "offended is harder to be won than a strong city," and "contentions" between people "are like the bars of a citadel" (Proverbs 18:19).

Yes, beware of false leaders, but more deceitful than false prophets or teachers are our own hearts when they are offended (see Jeremiah 17:9). Are you living with an offended heart? If so, you are gradually slipping away from true Christianity, which is known for its agape love.

Dealing with an offended heart is vital in maintaining ongoing spiritual maturity. For this reason, we need to look again at the things that offend us.

False Expectations

Sometimes offenses come because we expect *people* to fulfill our lives rather than *God*. Unrealistic or exaggerated expectations inevitably will cause others to fall short and offend us. Some desire their spouse or pastor or friends to meet their every need. God may indeed use people to help us. At the deepest level, however, our souls were created to find security in God, not man. When the Almighty truly becomes our security, our peace flows from His love, wisdom and unlimited capabilities, and we can live comfortably with imperfect people around us.

Still, the very power of our expectations can choke out the sweetness of a personal relationship. Suppose that, instead of burdening people with our expectations, we simply learned to appreciate them for themselves—no strings attached. The fact is: Our loved ones are not under any obligation to fulfill our desires. If they do fulfill them it is their free choice, not our demands, that makes for a loving relationship.

Part of our problem is the affluent world in which we live. We are served by hundreds of nonhuman "slaves," remarkable mechanical devices created just to serve us. Our slaves do laundry, clean dishes, figure bookkeeping and entertain us. They carry us across town and country—and for all they do, we are offended if their service does not meet or exceed our expectations.

Yet your spouse, friends or pastor are not your slaves. Our loved ones did not come with money-back guarantees. We did not buy them and we cannot trade them for newer models. This may come as a shock, but we do not own our loved ones.

Some people act as though they signed contracts with their spouses, such as they would with carpenters or plumbers—do such and such or you will not be paid. If you are an employer, a teacher or one who trains and holds people accountable, certain expectations are reasonable, but personal relationships are different. What I am saying is this: Instead of expecting my spouse to love and serve me, what if I put the demand upon myself to love and serve her, with no strings attached?

You think, *But we said vows together. I expect my spouse to fulfill what was promised.* What if she is fulfilling her vows to the best of her ability, but you cannot even discern her efforts because you are looking for something else? I am not saying there should not be times when we openly and honestly talk about our relationships. Certainly open communication is helpful. But what if we put the weight of the burden to change upon ourselves instead of our spouses?

Jesus said the greatest among us would be servant of all (see Matthew 23:11; Mark 10:43–44). We in our modern world have things reversed—we are the ones who are supposed to be the slaves. It is only our pride that thinks otherwise.

Suppose that a husband, instead of expecting a full-course dinner from his wife each night, learned to appreciate whatever she was able to offer him? Then instead of his failed expectation becoming an offense, there would be a living, sincere appreciation for the food his wife prepared. I know we have arrangements by common consent, but in reality a wife is under no obligation to cook special meals or do housekeeping. You did not marry her to be your housekeeper, but to become one with her.

Or imagine a husband who works at a long, tiring job. His wife, however, expects that he will work another two hours at home or go shopping with her or listen attentively to her problems. What if instead she welcomed him at the door and sincerely thanked him for daily giving himself to support their family? What if she met him not with demands but with appreciation? Maybe she would even rub his shoulders when he came home and, because of love, prepare his favorite meal.

You see, expectations can seem to be legitimate parts of a relationship, but they can also cause us to be offended and disappointed when people fall short. We should approach personal relationships with only one expectation: to serve—a demand we should put upon ourselves, not others. Let us expect of ourselves to always show love and thanksgiving for whatever we receive from our loved ones. Beloved, if we did so, we would have many happy couples in our midst.

In the Church

I have been speaking of offenses in family relationships, but the Church is also a family. Our expectations of others in the Body of Christ also can be unrealistic or exaggerated. Once again, we are expecting *people* to fulfill our lives rather than *God*, and we become offended when they do not meet those expectations. If we as pastors and churches learned to appreciate each other without false expectations, then we would see great healing come to our congregations.

Yes, it is important that leaders themselves be equipped, encouraged and held accountable. Pastors, however, also need certain freedoms to guide their churches. Indeed, the vision of a local church resides principally in the office of the senior pastor. He or she may answer to a church board or district supervisor, but God puts a special grace in the pastor, which is given him or her to lead the church. This imperfect person, together with the leadership team, is the Lord's primary means of guiding the congregation.

But when we expect the pastor to act like someone we saw on Christian television, we begin to breed discontent, false expectations and offenses. When our pastor resists these expectations, often he is simply seeking to be true to the vision he feels the Lord has given him. When the discontented individuals react, an oppression is released against that leader that actually feels and works like witchcraft (see 1 Samuel 15:23).

This happened to me a number of years ago. Several people in the church began praying that I would become more like a famed television minister. Each week they sat right in the front row, critically comparing me to the famous teacher they enjoyed. These people were not evil; they were good Christians. But their disappointment with me was a source of oppression that stole my confidence and actually lessened my effectiveness.

Let me give you an example from the Bible: Elisha succeeded Elijah, yet initially he failed the expectations of the sons of the prophets. They were familiar with Elijah's ministry style. Elisha, however, seemed to be Elijah's opposite. The prophets asked Elisha to send them to find Elijah. Perhaps he was not dead, but only "on some mountain" (2 Kings 2:16). Elisha refused. The next verse says that they "urged him until he was ashamed." Of what was Elisha ashamed? Even though he had received a double portion of Elijah's spirit, he became ashamed that he was not more like Elijah.

Our failed expectations can make a pastor feel ashamed for who he is. Nothing will kill the flowing of the Holy Spirit like ongoing criticisms of your church leaders. Learn to appreciate them for the gifts God has given them; pray for them, that they may become more like Christ.

Remember: If your pastor is faithful to preach the Gospel week in and week out, if he serves the Lord by trying to minister to Christ's Church, then God accepts him and you should honor him. He is a gift from God.

Likewise, pastors, accept and love the flock in which the Lord has placed you. Do not compare them to other churches, but appreciate their uniqueness in God's eyes. These people will cause you to grow in ways you have not grown before, so thank God for them.

The psalmist wrote, "Those who love Your law have great peace, and nothing causes them to stumble" (Psalm 119:165). There is a place in God where—as we mature—we can possess Christ's perfect response to all things. If we, as pastors and congregations, put away false, unrealistic expectations and focus on becoming Christlike to one another, we will have great peace. Beloved, nothing will cause us to stumble.

> *Lord, grant me that new creation heart that can walk as Jesus walked through a world of offenses without stumbling. I want to see everything as an opportunity to pray, every- thing as an opportunity to become Christlike. Lord, help me to interpret offenses as oppor- tunities that lead to transformations. Grant me, Lord Jesus, the pulse and beat of Your unoffendable heart. Amen.*

Satan's Hour

There is no greater opportunity to become Christlike than in the midst of pain and injustice. When Satan is raging with evil, God is planning to turn it to good. If we maintain our integrity in battle, if we let love rise to its purest expression, then we will touch the heart of God. Such is the path to our Father's power.

As we near the end of this book my prayer is that we will have eliminated a number of the vulnerabilities to—and effects of—church splits and other ungodly divisions. At the same time I realize that we can do almost everything right as pastors, leaders and churches and still suffer divisions. For some of us this actually may be part of God's greater plan for our lives—that we should endure rejection, conflict and slander as part of the process of becoming truly Christlike.

A Collective Madness

If you are part of a group that is engaged in splitting a church, my earnest admonition is that you flee quickly from the dividing group. If you do not heed my warning and instead fully embrace the resolve to split your church, a type of "collective madness" will occur. You will know what you are doing is wrong but will become so hardened that you detach yourself from guilt. You will be aware that your anger is venomous and un-Christlike, but you will be powerless to mute your words.

Beloved, no one needs to slay love to defend truth. Love is not truth's enemy; it is its validator. If what you say cannot be said in love, do not say it. It is not of God. To speak without love is evidence that the collective madness has begun to infect your soul.

A Visitation from Hell

Let us isolate this terrible insanity that drives people to say and do things they know are wrong. For the sake of discernment we shall call this season of madness "Satan's hour." It is a period of time when the restraining powers of all that is good seem to withdraw from human relationships. Instead of love—or even civility—what governs the dissenting group is the manifest "power of darkness" (Luke 22:53). It is as though people invite the legions of hell to depart the abode of the damned and find access to their secret resentments—the unresolved issues that exist in their hearts. Those things that are evil within human nature are fully awakened and then empowered by hell to fulfill every demonic gratification.

This collective madness is the exact opposite of a visitation from heaven; it is a visitation from hell. It is not the healing of bodies but the wounding of hearts. It is not reconciliation between souls but estrangement of friends. It is not truth spoken in love but emotions discharged in wrath. It is not the Gospel of peace but the heartache of strife. During Satan's hour friends become enemies, loyalties become betrayals and unity degrades into irreconcilable division. Satan's hour is an uncontested, seemingly unstoppable invasion from hell where every hidden jealousy and every secret, unresolved bitterness in the human heart is unsheathed and used as a weapon in the hands of demons of strife.

During His last few days on earth, Jesus Himself watched this invasion from hell advance upon the people of Jerusalem, infecting even His own disciples. If we study the terrible, demonic events that were compressed into Jesus' final earthly days, we gain vital insight into the demonic activity in church splits. And more importantly we can see how God can bring victory through it.

What Jesus Endured

This swarm of evil did not take Jesus unawares. Throughout His ministry Jesus frequently warned His disciples that a time of unfettered evil would come (see Mark 8:31; 9:12; Luke 17:25). As the day arrived, Jesus announced to His disciples that the hour of darkness was at hand (see John 14:30). Knowing a time of satanic darkness would come did not make it less painful, but having such insight helped Jesus to prepare.

Jesus was completely aware that during Satan's hour evil would strike in full force and His disciples would be sifted severely (see Luke 22:31). He knew His followers would scatter and one of the twelve would betray Him. Indeed, even His closest friends would deny they ever knew Him (see Luke 22:60–61). Satan's hour was a time when reality itself seemingly bent in service to the power of darkness (see Luke 22:53), and the Father offered nothing Jesus could use to stop it.

We cannot help but picture Jesus always upbeat and overcoming, but when hell was unleashed, even God's Son was not invulnerable to Satan's oppression. "Grieved and distressed," Jesus took His closest friends aside and spoke intimately with them about His heartache (see Matthew 26:37).

"My soul is deeply grieved, to the point of death," He said as He urged His closest friends, Peter, James and John, to keep watch with Him. Yet the heaviness of satanic battle overwhelmed them. Even John, who had rested his head on Jesus' breast, could not lift his head from slumber. All escaped into sleep, hiding themselves from excessive sorrow (see Matthew 26:38–45).

Staggered by the weight of the spiritual attack against Him, Jesus "fell to the ground and began to pray that if it were possible, the hour might pass Him by" (Mark 14:35). We know Jesus ministered peace wherever He went, yet now His intense, internal struggle ruptured blood vessels on His face, which beaded on His skin. Again He sought to waken His disciples. Roused from their sleep, they saw the droplets of blood on His brow and cheeks; still they could not endure.

I think it is significant that Jesus, so familiar with simply trusting His Father in all things, returned to His friends three times during the hour of His Gethsemane prayer (see Matthew 26:39–45). Beloved, there are some agonies in life for which God alone seems not enough; we crave also the comfort of our friends (see Proverbs 17:17). There is no substitute for God, yet our souls also need the embrace of a loyal companion, the shoulder of a faithful friend who has become closer than a brother.

Jesus' friends, however, were not there for Him. They slept while He prayed. They fled when the Pharisees came (see Matthew 26:56). During the trial when they—of all people—certainly could have defended Jesus' character and doctrine, they hid. Even if others would forsake Him, surely these who broke bread with Him—who knew His heart—would speak in His defense. Yet from Gethsemane to the cross Jesus heard the voice of just one friend. Peter, who less than a day earlier had sworn undying loyalty, now swore he never knew Him (see Matthew 26:69–70; Luke 22:60–61).

Our Master experienced betrayal, abandonment, slander, mockery and gross injustice. He endured the heartache of His disciples' failures—to pray, to stand and to defend the truth about their most wonderful friend and Lord.

Dear follower of Jesus, what our Messiah endured and what the disciples suffered in various degrees all are the elements found in a church split. What happens to a pastor or leader—what might have happened to *your* pastor during a church split—is similar in nature to what Jesus Himself suffered in His last few days.

How Jesus Overcame

For a leader, only one way points out of the tragedy of a church split: Become like Jesus. God's greatest goal for our lives is not that we become successful ministers, but that we become Christlike. Leading is simply an opportunity to be transformed into Christlikeness. This does not mean we must die for the sins of the world, but it does mean that when we go through injustices and conflicts, Christ must be manifested in our mortal lives.

What I mean by "manifesting Christ in our lives" is that we learn to respond to the human failures in our world as Jesus did in His. The wounding that strikes a pastor during a split comes through several sources. One of the worst is the apparent failure of church members and friends to speak in his defense. Confusion, fear and doubt can overshadow a congregation, even those who know better, paralyzing them into inaction. To counteract His disciples' failure, and knowing they, too, were being sifted, Jesus assured them, "But I have prayed for you, that your faith may not fail; and you, when once you have turned again, strengthen your brothers" (Luke 22:32).

There were valuable lessons for Jesus' disciples that only failure could teach, and Jesus knew this. These disciples had been arguing among themselves which of them might be the greatest; now they were humbled, broken and contrite enough for God to use them. God used their failure to excavate their souls of pride; now emptied, they were capable of being filled with the Holy Spirit. These same disciples would soon be willing to suffer and die for Jesus—and count it an honor to do so. They never denied Him again. Knowing they would fail Him, Jesus prayed that during their trial their faith would not fail and that upon returning they would become a strength for others.

The disciples' greatest problem was carrying the burden of their failure. Their guilt and condemnation weighed heavily upon them. Yet immediately after warning them that they each would, in fact, deny Him, Jesus comforted them, "Let not your heart be troubled" (John 14:1, KJV). Incredibly, even before they fell, Jesus sought to remove the weight of condemnation that inevitably would seek to overwhelm them.

So, friends, as Jesus loved His disciples, even though they failed Him, so we need to love those who, though falling short of our expectations, still remain with us. They will strengthen others. We need to remove any sense of condemnation or blame from those who have disappointed us. As they see our Christlike reactions they, too, will become united to serve God's highest purposes.

How Jesus Handled His Enemies

Jesus loved His disciples, and His love brought them through. But what about those people who played the role of the enemy, those who were instruments of injustice, who sought to destroy Jesus' ministry through gossip and slander? We must find Christ's reaction to these and emulate His behavior.

While Jesus had many legitimate arguments to wage against His accusers, He stood silently before them. In this example Christ shows us that there is a time to take your stand and defend what God is doing, and there is a time to become silent and simply entrust yourself to God. Peter reveals how Jesus processed the storm of accusation that came against His soul. Peter writes, "While being reviled, He did not revile in return; while suffering, He uttered no threats, but kept entrusting Himself to Him who judges righteously" (1 Peter 2:23). If your words will not persuade your attackers, beloved, recognize it is time to be silent.

Yet Jesus was not just silent. He bore their sins on His cross (see 1 Peter 2:24). When facing a storm of accusation, it is not enough that we not react negatively; we must respond positively to those who come against us, just as Christ did. We must pray the mercy prayer, even when it may appear that they have successfully put to death our vision.

You see, Jesus knew Satan's hour was coming. But He also knew that if He could maintain His vision of redemption and His capacity to love, it would be through this very time of darkness that redemption would triumph for mankind. Though grieved and deeply troubled, Jesus prayed, "What shall I say, 'Father, save Me from this hour'? But for this purpose I came" (John 12:27).

Jesus understood that for redemption to be accomplished, His love would face its most severe test. Jesus knew this battle was over one thing: Would He allow love to reach full maturity and its most perfect expression? Would He maintain His passion for man's redemption even as men mocked and crucified Him?

So it is with us. God allows injustices to perfect our love. The cross is the cost we pay so love can triumph. This battle is not about you and your enemies. It is about your choosing to maintain love in the midst of injustice.

Dear follower of Christ, let us redefine our meaning of success. Here is the success that will bring the power of redemption into our world: When we have endured Satan's hour and allowed adversity to refine our love, we will have succeeded in the purpose of our existence.

Beloved, regardless of the test God calls you to endure, it is not about you and your relational opponent. The real issue is about you and God. Will you allow love to be perfected? Will you transform Satan's hour into an offering of your life in Christlike surrender?

> *Lord Jesus, my soul longs and even yearns to*
> *be like You. Master of all that is good, grant*
> *me grace to succeed in love. Guard my heart*
> *from its natural instinct for self-survival. Let*
> *me never choose the way of hardness; let me*
> *in all things find the way of life. Even now,*
> *I offer myself for those who have struck me.*
> *Thank You for the opportunity to become like*
> *You. Amen.*

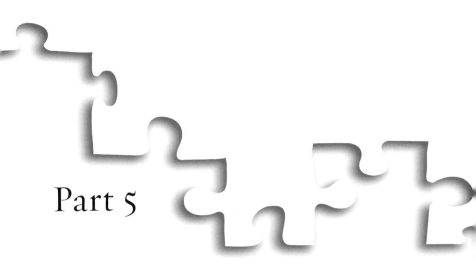

Part 5

The Gate of Heaven

"How awesome is this place!
This is none other than
the house of God,
and this is the gate of heaven."

Genesis 28:17

The House Is the
Gate of Heaven

A time will come when God's people shall manifest the oneness for which Jesus prayed concerning His Church. These saints will honor one another, even enjoying the different expressions of grace God has given each one. They will possess Christ-centered oneness with other Christians in their cities. They will introduce to their communities the very life of heaven.

We have discussed division, splits and the effects that selfish ambition have had upon unity in the Body of Christ. Let me add that the Lord has set His heart to end racism within the church as well. The Spirit of God has determined to remove the scourge of racial pride and division until we are truly our brothers' keepers. Even now, white people are repenting deeply of the history of prejudice we have exercised and tolerated in our culture.

You see, there are spiritual treasures hidden in the field
of cultural diversity within the Body of Christ. God has
planted unique graces in the African American community, without which the white church will never fulfill its
potential. He has given virtues to the Hispanic and Native
American churches that will unlock revival in cities. God
will use minorities to bring healing to regions; these graces
must be multiplied for us all to attain our destiny. Indeed,
a time is coming, I believe, when even the phrases "white
church" or "black church" or "Hispanic church" will become distant, outdated realities as we cross-pollinate with
one another. God's kingdom consists of Christians from
"every nation, people, tribe and tongue" (see Revelation
7:9)—all of whom are united in the Spirit of Jesus Christ.
Religious and cultural pride will evaporate in the red-hot
love of God. We will truly become one with each other in
Christ.

Thus, in spite of our historic divisions, I am convinced
that God will absolutely have a people who will overcome
the conflicts and divisions sown by the enemy. Unity of the
faith is possible because our great ally in this quest is the
Lord Jesus Himself. Not only is He praying for us, but our
unity in the last days has been foretold since ancient times.
Before the Lord returns, His united, spiritual "house" shall
be established on a worldwide scale. As it is written, "In
the last days the mountain of the house of the LORD will
be established as the chief of the mountains, and will be
raised above the hills; and all the nations will stream to
it" (Isaiah 2:2).

Even now the unfailing Word of God is coming to pass.
Throughout the Body of Christ, leaders and intercessors
are uniting in unprecedented ways. Do not doubt, in spite
of temporary setbacks, that the house of the Lord is being
restored. How significant is this? Today more than at any
other time since the first century, Christians from a variety
of backgrounds are uniting. We are learning to appreciate

our distinctions, not divide over them! Today the Spirit of God is establishing His house.

Some would argue that this unity is a prelude to the "one world church" of the Antichrist. Yet how can this be? The unity among Christians is for the cause of Christ; it involves prayer, love and humility—all the very ingredients the Lord requires for revival (see 2 Chronicles 7:14).

Others contend that the emergence of the house of the Lord will not occur until after Christ returns in the Millennium. Isaiah, however, plainly says God's house will be rebuilt "in the last days." The book of Acts identifies this era as having begun at Pentecost (see Acts 2:17). Thus, the time frame to which Isaiah's prophecy is referring is not the millennial age but our present dispensation.

I am amazed by the power in Isaiah's promise. He says all nations will stream to the mountain of the house of the Lord. *Only in God can streams flow up a mountain!*

This promise speaks of resurrection life being poured out upon nations—drawing people out of the ancestral sins and generational curses that have for so long weighed oppressively upon them. Supernatural power is coming from God to reverse the "gravity" of life's situations and create an updraft of hope and new beginnings!

Isaiah continues, "And many peoples will come and say, 'Come, let us go up to the mountain of the LORD, to the house of the God of Jacob; that He may teach us concerning His ways and that we may walk in His paths'" (Isaiah 2:3). This, too, is happening in our day. While some may be focusing on the world and the frightening signs of the times, still others are seeking to go deeper—to learn God's ways and to walk in His paths.

"For the law will go forth from Zion and the word of the LORD from Jerusalem. And He will judge between the nations, and will render decisions for many peoples" (Isaiah 2:3–4).

The Lord is rendering "decisions for many peoples" from His house. There are many conflicts between cultures in our world, yet the Lord compels us to deal with the issues and remedy them. Indeed, He has decreed: Racism and divisions cannot exist in God's house. As a result, reconciliation between races among born-again Christians has accelerated in recent years. Repentance is the first sign of revival; reconciliation is the fruit of revival.

"And they will hammer their swords into plowshares and their spears into pruning hooks" (Isaiah 2:4). What are plowshares and pruning hooks? They are instruments of the harvest. Once we renounce using our swords and spears against one another, we can work together to gather the harvest.

How Awesome Is This Place!

People argue that the end of the age will be full of the wrath of God. Yes, destructive judgments will come upon the world before Christ returns. But an outpouring of redemptive mercy also is coming from the Lord, and it will come streaming through His house into the world.

> "For behold, the day is coming, burning like a furnace; and all the arrogant and every evildoer will be chaff; and the day that is coming will set them ablaze," says the LORD of hosts, "so that it will leave them neither root nor branch. But for you who fear My name, the sun of righteousness will rise with healing in its wings."
>
> Malachi 4:1–2

Yes, wrath is coming, but so is healing. The Antichrist will arise, but so will the "sun of righteousness," and He will "rise with healing in [His] wings." For too long we have been focused only on the darkness at the end of the age. The saints, however, will experience the glory of God's Son, manifested and unveiled within His unified, living house (see Isaiah 60:1–3, 7)!

It is significant that Isaiah's prophecy about the restoration of God's house refers to it as "the house of the God of Jacob" (Isaiah 2:3). It was Jacob to whom the first revelation of God's house came. We may think God should have chosen one more spiritual. Jacob was fleeing Esau, whom he defrauded. Yet there is a message in this first unveiling of God's house: God chooses, redeems and transforms whom He wills (see Romans 9:18). Those He draws into His house, He absorbs into His craftsmanship.

The Scripture says, "[Jacob] had a dream, and behold, a ladder was set on the earth with its top reaching to heaven; and behold, the angels of God were ascending and descending on it. And behold, the LORD stood above it" (Genesis 28:12–13). Consider this about the character of the Lord's house: *It is the place where religion fades and the reality of God appears.* On all the earth, the house of the Lord is where God has chosen to dwell and manifest Himself.

"Then Jacob awoke from his sleep and said, 'Surely the LORD is in this place, and I did not know it.' He was afraid and said, 'How awesome is this place! This is none other than the house of God, and this is the gate of heaven'" (Genesis 28:16–17).

Beloved, for many reasons, what Jacob proclaimed continues to define us today. He said the Lord's house is "the gate of heaven." When the Church is humble, believing, loving, holy and united, there is absolutely no place on earth like the house of the Lord! It is truly an "awesome" place. *Indeed, we will never succeed in toppling the gates of hell until we first unite and become the gate of heaven.*

Jacob called this angelic reality, this spiritual abode where God and man could dwell together, *Bethel*, "the house of God" (see Genesis 28:19). It speaks of more than the visitation of God; this is His habitation.

The Highest Priority

Throughout the Old Testament, the people's regard for the house of the Lord actually revealed their regard for God Himself. In ancient times the Lord's house was a physical building, whether it was referred to as the tabernacle, sanctuary or temple. In the New Testament God's house is the Church (see 1 Corinthians 3:16; Hebrews 3:6). Yet under both old and new covenants the focus of the Lord was always upon the condition of His house.

Consider the importance the Bible itself places upon God's house: There are basically two chapters devoted to the details of the earth's creation, and there are several hundred references devoted to the details, construction, ceremony and significance of the house of the Lord. Clearly the service of the Lord's house rises far above nearly all other themes in the Old Testament!

The Father's house was to be a house of prayer, which would open the "gate of heaven." Its focus was not only to provide for the needs of Israel, but also to provide a place of intercession that would bring mercy to all nations. In this place, sacrifice was brought and forgiveness found; it was here that celebration and thanksgiving were offered. Even in Israel's times of national shame and exile, the Lord's house was to remain the center of Jewish peace. Indeed, after the dedication of the temple the Lord spoke to Solomon in a dream (see 2 Chronicles 7:12) and promised that as the Jews would "pray toward this place" (2 Chronicles 6:20, 21, 26), He would hear their prayer and restore them to their land (see 2 Chronicles 7:14). It was toward this very house, even in its devastated condition in Jerusalem, that Daniel opened his window and prayed three times a day (see Daniel 6:10). Amazingly the promise of God was that His "eyes and . . . heart will be there perpetually" (2 Chronicles 7:16).

In modern times we associate revival with increased miracles or signs, but biblically speaking if you wanted revival you began by rebuilding the house of the Lord. The greatest encouragement we have for a spiritual awakening is that in the Old Testament revival *always* followed the rebuilding of the house of the Lord. If we are serious about revival, at some point we must put away our divisions and embrace rebuilding the house of the Lord.

One may argue that the example of the Old Testament temple does not apply to New Testament Christians. Certainly we are not seeking to rebuild the Jewish Temple— although that would indeed be a revival of sorts. Our focus is not on a building made with hands but the spiritual union created by believers united in Christ. Paul tells us that today the Body of Christ is God's living temple on earth (see 1 Corinthians 3:16). Thus, the *principles* and *priorities* that determined revival in the Old Testament are perfectly applicable to us in our times.

Today we are praying and working for revival in our land. If we would give the restoration of the Lord's house a higher priority, if we would repair our ruined relationships and rebuild our fallen unity, then we would find an ever-increasing power from God to heal our national needs. We will never have the manifestation of heaven touching earth without first restoring the house of the Lord. God's house is the gate of heaven.

> *Master, our unity exists because You exist*
> *and our lives are rooted in You. Blessed Lord,*
> *forgive us for tolerating disunity. Grant us*
> *Your eyes, Your love, and Your faith to see the*
> *Church as You see it: the gate of heaven on*
> *earth! Amen.*

The River Runs
through It

Our days are not unlike the days of Ezra, Nehemiah, Zechariah and Malachi, where the work of rebuilding God's temple hit stages, faced battles and delays but continued into national restoration. Beloved, the healing God has for society at large rises from and flows out of the house of the Lord.

In recent years the Holy Spirit has inspired godly leaders to turn and begin rebuilding God's house. Relationships between denominations and races have experienced new levels of healing, respect and reconciliation. This move toward spiritual harmony, while it may seem to ebb and flow, has progressively unfolded into a genuine restoration of unity in the born-again Church.

As a leader I have been privileged to be invited to many church leadership meetings on both national and international levels. I can say without hesitation that God has been leading every major, born-again Christian leader I know, whether from evangelical or Pentecostal traditions, to work toward greater unity with other born-again Christians. If you recall where the Church was in the beginning of the 1980s, you will see the trend toward unity is obvious and profound.

We are making progress. Thus, I believe a great awakening for our land is on God's calendar. The prophet Ezekiel's words illumined what has been occurring. In chapters 40 through 43, Ezekiel foresaw a time when the house of the Lord would be rebuilt, also restoring God's glory to the land (see Ezekiel 43:1–6). The chapters that follow continue speaking of the restoration, but then in chapter 47, Ezekiel records an amazing event: "From under the threshold of the house . . . from south of the altar" water was flowing (verse 1).

This water was but a trickle at first. Then it flowed ankle deep, then knee deep; soon it reached the loins and continued rising until it became a river that could not be forded. Ezekiel tells us that wherever the river went, it brought life and healing (see verses 8–9, KJV). *It is important to see that the river did not flow straight from heaven; it came through the rebuilt house of the Lord!*

Today on a worldwide scale the river of God's life is truly flowing into many nations of the world. It is not happening coincidentally but as a direct result of Christians coming together as the Lord's house. Some will say, "Wait! The Church is not completely united. We still are divided in many ways." True. And others will say the river is still quite shallow. That is also true.

The depth of the river that flows out of the temple is proportional to the depth of our unity!

Just as the Lord is not finished uniting us, so the river is not finished rising. Imagine, therefore, the power of the river of God when the Lord is finished building His house.

Remember: In the last days this glorious house will be "established as the chief of the mountains" (Isaiah 2:2).

As we continue to unite as the Lord's living house, the river will rise accordingly. The sign of revival is that the house of the Lord is rebuilt. The house is the gate of heaven; the river runs through it.

Lord, give me Your vision of the importance of unity. Help me to recognize that what You are building among Your people is not merely a religion about You but a dwelling for You. Master, return to our corporate lives and flow into our world through us! Amen.

Becoming the Answer to Christ's Prayer

When we give ourselves in love, in intercession, in good deeds, in humble and joyful service to help unite God's people, we are actually increasing the pleasure in Christ's heart. Our unity fulfills the intercessory prayer of the Son of God!

"Show me in the Bible," the pastor urged. "Show me where God says our different churches are supposed to be united."

I tried to restrain myself, but it was not easy. I did not want to overwhelm him with the hundreds of Scriptures that call us, either directly or indirectly, to unity with other born-again Christians.

I had heard this complaint before. According to the theology of my new acquaintance, to say, "Okay, I'll unite in prayer with other pastors," was tantamount to saying, "Yes,

I'll join the One World Church and follow the Antichrist."
In his mind, any unity with other churches was blatantly
false; it meant closing his eyes and being swallowed up in
the "great falling away."

I took a deep breath. Over the years I have come to realize
that often when people study the Bible, instead of actually
believing what they read, their perception narrows so that
they see only what they already believed. So in addition to
using just the right text, I really needed the wisdom and
gentleness of Christ.

Should I use the book of Romans, where Paul provided a
variety of ways to bring Jewish and Gentile Christians into
unity (see Romans 3:22–23, 29; 4:16–17; 5:16–19; 6:5; 12; 14;
16)? Or should I reference 1 and 2 Corinthians, where Paul
rebukes Christians for their divisions (see 1 Corinthians
1:10–13; 3:1–4, 21–23; 2 Corinthians 12:20–21) while also
calling the Church to its highest diversity and harmony
(see 1 Corinthians 12–14)?

So much of the New Testament is given to the subject of
unity that it was difficult to decide. I did not have much
time so I went right to John 17, which not only talks about
the unity of Christians but also reveals the heart of Christ
as He Himself pleads for oneness among His people.

"Do you think the Scripture is true," I asked, "that
'Jesus Christ is the same yesterday and today and forever'
(Hebrews 13:8)?" He answered affirmatively. "And would
it be safe to imagine, since Jesus ever lives to make intercession for the Church, that He would be praying for many
of the same things today that He asked for in the first century?" (See Romans 8:27; Hebrews 7:25.) Again he agreed.
I then asked him to turn to the gospel of John.

To truly study Jesus' prayer in John 17 is to step into His
heart. Here we discover that in spite of His disciples' fears
and ambitions Jesus still required them to be united. Their
unity was not merely an ecclesiastical thing; He wanted
them to actually be known for their uncommon love for

one another. This love and unity would be the confirming mark that would cause all men to recognize them as true followers of Israel's Messiah.

Remember: These were the same men who were known to argue about their positions and compete as to which should be considered greatest. They were frequently subject to carnal ideas and hidden agendas, often not realizing in the least what Jesus meant when He taught. Yet Jesus did not abandon His disciples, even though they were carnal, ambitious and divided. Rather, He was committed to them from start to finish. He did not sanction their divisions or pretend their discord did not exist. Instead He prayed for their unity and asked that their vision of oneness be lifted to the standard of the Godhead!

I told my friend that today this same Spirit of Christ, the One we bow before and call "Lord," pleads for our unity as well. He is the same yesterday, today and forever. My question is: How can we be so deaf to His desires, so cold toward His passions? How can we say we love Him and not keep His commandments or embrace His vision for us?

Our Divisions Are the Devil's Attack against Jesus

It is Satan who seeks to take our focus off Jesus. The devil manipulates our natural and cultural distinctions and turns them into reasons to divide from other born-again Christians. The divisions that pit born-again Christians against each other must be discerned for what they truly are: part of the larger conflict between Satan and the Lord Jesus. *The devil cannot touch the Lord directly, but he can exploit our discord to bring pain to the heart of Christ.*

Yes, we must make room for diversity of expression in our churches; we must defend the right for congregations to have different callings in God. Yet we must not allow these things to divide us. There are times when Christians think they are defending the truth, when in fact they are dividing over style or emphasis. Again, I am not saying we should end our denominations, just our divisions between born-again Christians.

It is amazing to me how Satan has convinced so many Christians that unity with other believers is evil! If ever there was a false doctrine so widespread, so accepted in the Body of Christ yet so contrary to the heart and teachings of Christ, it is the tradition of division within the Church!

Of course, my minister friend is correct not to unite with every so-called Christian or church organization. There are many false Christians. Satan still masquerades as an angel of light. Yet in my opinion, the question is not whether or not we will be led astray and become false; the challenge today is if we will repent of the unbiblical divisions among born-again Christians and finally become true!

The Source of True Unity

Upon what basis should we build unity? In John 17 Jesus gave us three dynamics, three fundamental truths, which He said would lead His Church into the most profound state of unity—oneness such as the Father and Son enjoyed. That state of divine unity would be accessed by our correctly relating to Christ's name, His Word and His glory.

First, here is what Jesus prayed concerning the oneness produced by His name: "Holy Father, keep them in Your name, the name which You have given Me, that they may be one even as We are" (John 17:11). God calls us into unity with all those who, like us, have called upon the name of the Lord. This is a wide umbrella, and the unity here is not based upon common interpretation of peripheral doctrinal positions but on a common need for God's help and forgiveness. The fact is that we are already united under the redemptive power of Christ's name. All who call upon the

Lord will be saved. If we have called upon Jesus Christ, then all of us are united in needing Him. This is not something to attain but to acknowledge and accept, for at the foot of His cross we are one.

But if the name of Jesus has given us a *positional* oneness, the words of Jesus bring us into *functional* oneness. Here again Jesus defined the conditions that create unity. He prayed, "I do not ask on behalf of these alone, but for those also who believe in Me through their word; that they may all be one" (John 17:20–21).

We are united in His name, but we are also united through His Word. When Jesus prays for unity in His Church, He does not make the source of that unity man's innate ability to organize himself around projects, structures or ideals. He says that it is through His "word," which His apostles lived, transcribed and proclaimed, that "those who believe . . . may . . . be one."

When Christ refers to the Word, He is actually speaking of the testimony of two things. The first proclaims what Jesus did, thus establishing the reality of His redemptive mission in all who believe. This is our testimony of redemption, the new covenant and the cross. Yet Jesus is also speaking of the continuation and replication of His life, which is manifested and defined in His teaching. If we do not have oneness with another born-again Christian, it is probably because one or both of us are not following Jesus' words. It is His Word that creates oneness in the lives of those who now follow Him. The continuation of His doctrine was the very heart of the Great Commission (see Matthew 28:19–20).

Christ's life, as it is embodied in both His redemptive mission and His teaching, is the foundational reality upon which all of Christianity is constructed. His sacrifice atones for our past; His Word establishes and creates our future. It is here that true oneness and Christian discipleship emerge.

The last stage of unity, however, is perhaps the highest and most wonderful. Indeed, the first two stages of unity—His name and His Word—prepare the inner sanctuary of our hearts for the great purpose of our existence: to be indwelt by the spiritual presence of Christ Himself. Jesus refers to this living presence as His glory. He said, "The glory which You have given Me I have given to them, that they may be one, just as We are one; I in them and You in Me, that they may be perfected in unity, so that the world may know that You sent Me, and loved them, even as You have loved Me" (John 17:22–23).

"I in them and You in Me, that they may be perfected in unity." The Greek word for *unity* here means "into a unit." This is the height and goal of true Christianity—the revelation of Jesus Christ through His Church. We receive provisional oneness through His name, functional oneness through His Word, and living, radiant oneness through His indwelling presence. This hope of oneness is not something that will happen only in the sweet by-and-by, but something that is to be so explicitly manifested here that even "the world may believe" in the power and person of Christ (John 17:21).

We Can Answer His Prayer

This book has been an appeal for unity and spiritual oneness in the Church of Jesus Christ. We have exposed the demonic root that is the source of many of our divisions; we have set before our eyes the lofty goal of oneness in the Church.

Let me add one concluding thought. We all can agree that Jesus Himself is the one answer to our earthly problems. If I ask for guidance, He is my Shepherd; if I am sick, He is my Healer. When I am perplexed, He is my Teacher and Counselor. He gave Himself so He might become everything to me. But there is something we can give back to our wonderful Savior. We can be the answer to His prayer for unity.

Each time we choose to pray for others instead of merely criticizing them, we are answering His prayer. Every time we turn and forgive a brother or sister who has hurt us, we are fulfilling His longing. When we unite with other churches across racial or denominational lines, we are touching His heart. Think of it. As small and otherwise ordinary as we are, we can be the answer to His prayer: "Father, make them one."

Dear Jesus, I want to be an answer to Your prayer. Help me to access oneness with You by correctly relating to Your name, Your word and Your glory. Then use me as an instrument of Your love to unite Your Church. Amen.

Appendix 1

The Deception Surrounding Church Splits

The Bible has a great deal to say about unity. I have yet to find one New Testament example, however, where the Scriptures encourage born-again Christians to divide from each other. The Lord *multiplied* the church and *added* to their numbers (see Acts 2); He did not divide His people.

Let the Word Be True

For more than 35 years I have witnessed many Scriptures taken out of context and twisted to suit the purpose of division. Yet if we simply read objectively, we will not find one place where the Spirit of God inspired a faction within a church to divide and start another group, even if the first group was imperfect.

Dividing a church has no scriptural precedent. Just as people are deceived in their motives when they divide Christ's Church, so they are deceived when they read the Scriptures seeking to justify themselves.

I have frequently heard quoted, for instance, Paul's admonition: "Come out from their midst and be separate" (2 Corinthians 6:17). The apostle, however, was not speaking of being separated from other Christians. Rather, his purpose was to warn Christians about being "unequally yoked" with pagans or "unbelievers" (see 2 Corinthians 6:14–15, KJV).

Interestingly, the Old Testament version of this same verse was used by the Pharisees to justify their condescending attitude toward other Jews. In fact, the name *Pharisee* literally translated means "the separate." Jesus warned of those who "trusted in themselves that they were righteous, and viewed others with contempt" (Luke 18:9). This attitude of self-righteous contempt is often what motivates a faction to think of itself as more spiritual than another, and thus justify being "separate."

Another historic misinterpretation comes from 1 Corinthians 11, where Paul seems to concede that splits and divisions were almost necessary. He wrote, "I hear that divisions exist among you; and in part I believe it. For there must also be factions among you, so that those who are approved may become evident among you" (1 Corinthians 11:18–19).

Certainly, isolated by itself, the idea that there "must also be factions . . . that those who are approved may become evident" adds legitimacy to the idea of splits and divisions. Of course, those who split from others always identify themselves as "those who are approved."

The actual context of the verse, however, reveals the apostle's true perception and view. Here is the complete eighteenth verse: "For, in the first place, when you come together as a church, I hear that divisions exist among you; and in part I believe it" (1 Corinthians 11:18).

Listen carefully to Paul's backdrop of unity upon which he isolates the problem of divisions. He introduces his thoughts by saying, "When you come together as a church. . . ." Do not rush past his opening address. They had not split from each other; they were not meeting in different buildings, each with a unique name on a corner sign. They were still united and they all still would "come together as a church." In fact, until the initial split between Constantinople and Rome two hundred years later, there was only the one Christian Church. Paul was not justifying the divisions among them. In fact, the primary theme of 1 Corinthians is to reestablish unity (see chapters 1, 3, 8, 10:16–24, 11, 12, 13, 14). He wrote specifically to *correct* their divisions. But even though, in their carnality, some were followers of Paul while others followed Apollos or Cephas, they still came "together as a church." Paul's goal in this letter was to get them to see past the leaders who brought them into the Kingdom and look at the King!

Every week the Christians in Corinth met together for worship, a love feast and weekly Communion. It was here in the administration of food that they broke into the cliques and factions that Paul identified as "approved." Some tried to keep their focus on the significance of the Lord's Supper, while others were devouring as much as they could during the community meal (see 1 Corinthians 11:20–22, 33–34)!

In no way had Paul suddenly altered his course and decided that divisions were not a bad thing after all. Rather, he was acknowledging that the more gluttonous Christians had become a separate group within the Church. In contrast, unintentionally, the Christians who reverently waited became a group as well. This was not by premeditated design or organizational intent but by their self-discipline and composure. Just as cream rises to the top of milk, so within the Church there were those whose spirituality gave contrast to the carnality of others—and those were the ones who were approved. But they did not divide from the others and form a new church within the Church. Paul did not urge them to separate from the others, for they all still came "together as a church."

In the very next chapter Paul reiterates his theme of unity, using the analogy of a body that is diverse, yet interdependently united. Everything he has written to this point is captured in his summary thought in verse 25. Listen again to his heart: "That there should be no schism in the body; but that the members should have the same care one for another" (1 Corinthians 12:25, KJV).

Beloved, the word translated *schism* in the King James (rendered *division* in the NASB), means "split" in the Greek language. Translated literally, Paul is saying, "There should be no split in the body."

What part of "no" do we not understand? Unity is the central theme of 1 Corinthians. How could one honestly ignore entire chapters about unity and take one half verse out of context to justify a split (see 1 Corinthians 11:18–19)? This is willful deception.

The Goal Is Unity

In all that the New Testament declares for Christians—in all of the epistles and pastoral letters of Paul and the other apostles—the call is clearly, unmistakably toward unity, not division. There was a hurricane of spiritual wind blowing and bending the Church in the direction of oneness with each other in Christ. The repeated rebuke comes because of disunity and sectarianism.

Another verse used to justify splitting a church comes from Jesus Himself. He said, "Do you suppose that I came to grant peace on earth? I tell you, no, but rather division" (Luke 12:51). Jesus is not talking about dividing His people but dividing those who follow Him from those who do not.

Jesus does indeed separate us from the world. He eternally unites us, however, to Himself and one another.

As I searched through the New Testament on the subject of Christian unity, hundreds of verses pointed toward oneness in the born-again Church. After years of study on this subject, I have yet to read one verse that instructed a group of Christians to slander, divide and split from another group of Christians in a city just because that other group was imperfect. If God's Word calls us to unity with other born-again Christians throughout an entire city, how much more does this same command apply to relationships in a local church?

Yet we need to realize that we all are different, with differing strengths and passions. Part of unity means we can accept that some people within our church community may desire to function differently than others. This diversity need not become disunity. We must defend the right to be unique, with differing tasks. But diversity must find its expression without contention or strife.

The test for leaders and congregations is to find creative ways to facilitate diversity while remaining united. If unity of purpose cannot be maintained within a body of people, a church plant born of love and done with wisdom in the Lord's timing is a creative possibility.

One Example of Multiplying a Church

Several years ago I approached one of our associate pastors at River of Life, Marty Boller, and asked if he was praying about moving out of state. He said, "Yes." Marty had been a Vineyard pastor who merged his congregation with us, and now seven years later he wanted to return to the Vineyard association of churches. Yet Marty did not want to sow division in our community, so he planned on moving to Canada to start his church!

Because he was an honorable man and committed to unity, I suggested he take a few months and explain his vision in a weekly class with those from our church who were interested. When Marty started a new work in our city, he did so with a dozen or so River of Life families and others. Today we remain great friends and serve together in many citywide projects. We are closer because he was patient, wise and nondivisive.

There are many creative ways to multiply a church as long as we stay Christlike. It is when pride or ambition enters that division soon follows.

A Purer First-Century Church?

The argument arises that the Church was much purer in its early years than it is now—so today we need to separate from others because of sin in the camp. The Church in Jerusalem, in its inception, certainly set a standard for us all. As the Church expanded to other cities and cultures, however, there were many problems; in some cases their failures were worse than our own. Yet the apostles who served Christ's Church still called for unity in spite of the churches' imperfections.

Even in Jesus' address to the seven churches in the Revelation of John, though sin existed in the churches in five cities, Christ never instructed the innocent to break from the sinners. Rather, He commended those who walked in purity and left them in the midst of the sinful as an example of His righteousness.

Doctrine

Another argument used to justify splits has to do with doctrinal interpretation. Let me make it clear that our doctrines are important—they define our belief systems and open the door to spiritual realities and levels of blessedness of which we otherwise would be ignorant. Having clear, biblically based doctrines also provides boundaries to keep us from deception and half-truths.

Our faith, however, consists of both core truths and peripheral truths. There are precepts that we must be willing to die for, yet there are other instructions that good Christians interpret differently. Because we are all learning, we must be willing to yield and stay humble.

In practical terms we cannot be united with those who do not believe in the deity of Christ. Yet we certainly can maintain the unity of the Spirit, for instance, with someone who has a different view about the timing of the Rapture. We cannot dilute God's truth concerning the New Covenant, the inspiration of the Scriptures, the centrality of Jesus Christ, the atonement of His cross, His bodily resurrection, His physical return, salvation by grace through faith, the Trinity and the indwelling work of the Holy Spirit. But we are still learning about spiritual gifts, effective church government, signs and wonders, styles of praise, and various programs that train youth and make disciples of adults.

When Jesus defined the requirements for unity in John 17, He said our oneness would arise from three core realities. He said spiritual oneness would come as we believed in His name, His Word and His glory (see John 17:11, 20–22). He said that these fundamental truths, if adhered to, would unite His people.

To split a church, however, because of a disagreement concerning peripheral doctrines is a smoke screen. It is a deception. There are those who argue they are taking their stand in defense of God's Word. Yet how can they divide a church in defiance of God's Word? A person who will split a church over a nonfundamental doctrine or over a spiritual gift or style of worship is deceived and seeking to deceive others.

> *Lord, forgive us for accepting divisions. Heal Your Church, O God! Bring us into Christ-centered unity, so the world will believe in Your power. In Jesus' name. Amen.*

Appendix 2

Questions and Answers

What exactly is a church split?

Generally speaking a split occurs when a group within a church, usually under the influence of an associate minister or worship leader, finds fault with the senior pastor's leadership. Usually the goal of the dissenting group is not merely change but control of the church. They are seeking power. If they cannot gain control of the church, they refine their organization, solidify their constituency and without the blessing of the parent church leave to start a new church in the community.

Is the pastor ever at fault in a split?

Yes. A split may occur when a church board hires (or "extends a call" to) a pastor whom they think will serve the vision of the church. If the church has been established for a number of years and the founding minister is no longer involved, there exists a unique authority within the church board. In a sense the deacons or elders serve that church as the "keepers of the vision." They are looking to maintain consistency between past leaders and present leaders. They expect change but also expect that the pastor who answers their call will respect their preferences.

Splits often occur when a minister hides his convictions concerning certain doctrines or spiritual gifts. Then when the board realizes this pastor has not been forthright with his intentions, the pastor either resigns or is fired. Unfortunately, there is usually a certain percentage of the church that has bonded with the pastor and may decide to leave with him to begin a new work in the same community. This is an unethical way to start a church.

Additionally, if a pastor falls into serious sin yet refuses to submit to discipline, the other leaders in that church have a moral responsibility to remove that pastor. If he refuses to submit to the church board, the elders of that church might start a new work, splitting from the pastor and those loyal to him. They have not sinned by leaving the pastor who refuses correction.

What about apostasy? Is it okay to split in that instance?

Another occasion when a split might become necessary occurs when the leaders of a denomination fall away from the faith and seek to spread their apostasy into their denomination. If senior church leaders deny the deity of

Christ or find no problem ordaining and endorsing homosexuals, or if they teach that all religions lead to God, this is a denomination that has turned its back on biblical Christianity. For a pastor to withdraw his or her congregation from that denomination is not sin, but a noble responsibility.

Before pulling out of that denomination, however, I would suggest that local church leadership seek out other pastors who are likewise resisting the downward spiral of their denomination. Perhaps pockets of godly pastors within the denomination also are combating the current trend away from godliness. Still, to withdraw from the denomination as a means of protest, especially to protect Christ's sheep, can be an honorable decision.

What about leaving a church? Would that be considered splitting?

If a person, family or even up to three or four families decide to transfer to another church, their actions should not be considered a split. People will always come and go, needing to be equipped by the variety of ministers Christ has throughout His church. People should be free to sense and fulfill the changing seasons in their lives. But they should make their transition with a minimum of rancor or contention. They also should be careful not to sow discontentment at their former church. Whenever possible, pastors should make a church transfer a positive experience for all, sending attendees to their next church with a blessing.

In the New Testament, apparently "letters of commendation" often accompanied Christians as they traveled between churches or cities (see 2 Corinthians 3:1). Communication is important. Today a simple phone call between pastors will do. If we are members of a church and plan on relocating to another church, it is simply a courtesy to communicate to your pastors and staff that you are moving. But to leave one congregation and go to another is part of our liberty in Christ.

Are there times of greater battle?

There will always be certain times when we are more vulnerable to strife and division. One such time occurs when a congregation is in a season of change. Trying to adjust to a new pastor or church training program, for example, calls for greater grace. A new worship leader may sing your favorite chorus differently. Or the deacon board's new building plan may strike you wrong. Even times of sudden growth can be disturbing to some, leaving them vulnerable to criticism and withdrawal.

Whatever the current transition is, there will always be those who think the old ways were better. In nearly every church, there will be "those who desire change" sitting side by side with "those who hate change." God puts both types of people in the same congregation to create flexibility and balance in all.

Yet as difficult as the transition is, remember: Satan will seek opportunities for division and strife. This is why we should honor our church leaders and pray for them. Their pace rarely pleases everyone.

What about the biblical admonition to God's people to come out of Babylon (see Revelation 18)?

My focus is on the relationship evangelical Christians have with one another, not Babylon. Within the born-again, Christ-trusting congregation of God, church splits are a sin that needs to be renounced.

What about splits over spiritual phenomena?

Spiritual phenomena should never be a reason a church divides, yet often the enemy is able to manipulate human reactions and use our own "sensibilities" against us. Certainly the ministry of prayer for God's people is consistent with the ministry of Jesus Himself. It is all the more powerful when God *answers* prayer with renewed spirits, minds and bodies. Let us defend laying hands upon the sick and praying for them. When certain signs begin to manifest, however, it is easy to "ritualize" the phenomena. The more extra-biblical in nature those phenomena are, the more likely Satan will make them divisive.

Generally speaking, a spiritual phenomenon can be categorized as that which is either biblical, extra-biblical or unbiblical. The manifestations accompanying New Age concepts, astrology, obsession with UFOs, "channeling," witchcraft and the like are obviously unbiblical. The Bible condemns these things, since the spiritual activity joined to them is demonic.

Biblical manifestations include anointed preaching (resulting in conviction, repentance or inspiration in the listener), physical or emotional healing, deliverance from demonic possession and the inspired "word" gifts: prophecy, tongues, words of knowledge and wisdom (see 1 Corinthians 12, 14). Even in the first century, however, conflict arose with the misuse of spiritual gifts. Although spiritual gifts are biblical in nature, their content should be tested against Scripture, their presentation should be done decently and in order, and any word of direction should be confirmed by two or three witnesses.

While the Lord is most clearly recognized in biblical manifestations—and most obviously not associated with what is unbiblical—difficulty comes when we encounter religious manifestations that have no pattern in the Bible.

These would be classified as extra-biblical, and it is around these signs that churches most often split.

I am not going to pass judgment on the legitimacy of any extra-biblical sign. I know a great many pastors who personally were restored during a time of spiritual renewal in which the Lord used an extra-biblical sign; I also know pastors who suffered severe nervous breakdowns because of the strife they experienced as they tried to shepherd a congregation through the turbulence generated by extra-biblical signs. I will simply suggest that pastors, after introducing the spiritual phenomena to their churches over a period of several weeks, add a monthly or biweekly Friday evening service that is geared just for this renewal, without seeking to conform the whole congregation to it. This way people will not be forced to be "with it" or "against it."

Speaking as one who has been in ministry for more than 35 years, I can tell you that spiritual phenomena will not be manifest in a congregation forever. You cannot build your church on signs and wonders. You must preach the Word and disciple your congregation. Make them followers of Jesus. If you are attending a church where making disciples of Jesus is the pastor's goal, do not split or divide that church over signs.

Our church started years ago as a result of a split. We have since suffered four splits ourselves and are currently in another one. How do we break this curse?

I suggest you contact the original church from which yours split and arrange a time when you can meet with the pastor. Together with your leadership team, ask your former pastor and his or her leaders for forgiveness for how your church was started. See if you can arrange to have a joint meeting between the two churches where the past can be forgiven and brought to the cross. You also might have Communion together and pledge to be one another's keeper. Make sure your congregation is fully aware of your repentance so they can join with you in breaking the pattern of division.

When a pastor is a controlling personality, how do you leave?

I am comforted by the fact that heaven is a big place with room for all sorts of people. For some of us strict leadership is hard to accept, but many people genuinely thrive under it. Certain people need clear rules, and a leader who communicates with strong authority is a help to them. Others, of course, feel completely smothered by this type of leader. They also find it difficult to leave without feeling excessive guilt or intimidation.

First, remember that you are free in Jesus. No man or woman on earth is your lord, and your pastor is your servant. You are completely at liberty to visit other places of worship. When you have found a new church home, contact your former pastor, thank him or her, and just move on as best you can.

If, however, the pastor is so controlling that he or she warns you will lose your salvation if you leave or threatens you with subtle curses, contact another pastor in your community and get counsel. You do not have to submit to such abuse, and neither should anyone else in that church.

If new wine must be put into new wineskins, it seems to me that sometimes splits are inevitable.

Again I think we need Jesus as our pattern. Jesus did not slander John the Baptist and work people out of his movement, which is what happens in a church split. In fact, when John's disciples saw that Jesus was baptizing more people than John and the Pharisees noticed the opportunity for strife, Jesus moved His ministry elsewhere, lest he cause division in the Kingdom of God (see John 4:1–6). As best I can tell, Jesus' other disciples were unattached to any group or movement in Israel. Jesus did not split a group to start His work; He is the pattern for the "new wine."

Recently our pastor and his staff came under a lot of criticism from the church board and were fired suddenly. Over the past years he had built our congregation to twice the size it first was. We have since started a new church and he is still our pastor. But I was wondering, was starting a new church wrong?

Assuming there was no serious sin involved, the dismissal of a pastoral staff seems harsh. I would encourage them, as the Lord leads and confirms the timing, to look for ways to heal the wounds between both groups. The best outcome of this situation is for each congregation to accept and respect each other's different preferences and forgive each other. Perhaps the Lord will provide a time when both groups can meet together with the Lord's Supper. To speak the blessing of the Lord over each other and release one another from the heartache of the past will go far in establishing healing.

My pastor's sermons have been dry and lifeless for quite a while. When we are not being fed the meat of God's Word, should we start our own church?

No teacher brings sermons that are "meat." Jesus said that His "meat" was to do the will of His Father (John 4:34, KJV). If your church seems dry and you are hungry for meat, I suggest you begin doing the will of God in your church. What I mean is that you start a prayer group for your pastor. Encourage him with comments about his sermon. Perhaps send him words of encouragement and build him up.

You say, "But this is what we want him to do for us." If you pray for him, more than likely he will begin to gain new confidence and become a great encouragement to you. But the real "meat" is this: See the need and be mature enough in Christ to pray, encourage and stand in faith until that need is met by the Holy Spirit.

Francis Frangipane currently serves as the senior pastor of River of Life Ministries in Cedar Rapids, Iowa. The author of twelve books, including *This Day We Fight!*, *The Three Battlegrounds* and *Holiness, Truth and the Presence of God*, he has also written a number of booklets, as well as a four-book set of manuals for In Christ's Image Training, an online school.

The Lord has used the Christ-centered teaching of Francis Frangipane, who is president of Advancing Church Ministries and who has been a pastor since 1971, to unite thousands of pastors in hundreds of cities around the world. His online training school has students from more than fifty nations. Additionally Francis' television ministry reaches people in more than two hundred nations.

Francis and his wife, Denise, live near Cedar Rapids, Iowa, and have five grown children.

In Christ's Image Training

In Christ's Image Training (ICIT), the online correspondence course Pastor Francis has developed, offers four opportunities for enrollment in Level I training each year: January, April, July and October.

Level I: Certification offers four foundational tracks: Christlikeness, humility, prayer and unity. Completion time, six months.

Level II: Leadership Training offers further online teaching by Pastor Francis and other national church leaders. Completion time, three months.

Level III: Facilitation and Commissioning provides spiritual equipping for those preparing for ministerial opportunities.

On-Site Impartation and Focused Training offers a three-day seminar that can be taken by attendance or via audio-tapes. See the website for details.

Association graduate students who desire ongoing association with other ICIT graduates, as well as fellowship with like-minded Christians and churches, are invited to become part of Advancing Church Ministries Association of Churches and Ministries.

In Christ's Image Training center is not a denomination, nor is Advancing Church Ministries (ACM). Please see the website for enrollment fees and detailed information.

To contact the ministries of Francis Frangipane, or for equipping material, write or visit:

Advancing Church Ministries
125 Robins Square Ct.
Robins, IA 52328-9650
Toll-free order line: (877) 363-6889
www.InChristsImage.org
www.arrowbookstore.com